asyncio Recipes

Mohamed Mustapha Tahrioui
Darmstadt, Hessen, Germany

ISBN-13 (pbk): 978-1-4842-4400-5   ISBN-13 (electronic): 978-1-4842-4401-2
https://doi.org/10.1007/978-1-4842-4401-2

Managing Director, Apress Media LLC: Welmoed Spahr
Acquisitions Editor: Celestin Suresh John
Development Editor: James Markham
Coordinating Editor: Aditee Mirashi

Cover designed by eStudioCalamar

Cover image designed by Freepik (www.freepik.com)

Distributed to the book trade worldwide by Springer Science+Business Media New York, 233 Spring Street, 6th Floor, New York, NY 10013. Phone 1-800-SPRINGER, fax (201) 348-4505, e-mail orders-ny@springer-sbm.com, or visit www.springeronline.com. Apress Media, LLC is a California LLC and the sole member (owner) is Springer Science + Business Media Finance Inc (SSBM Finance Inc). SSBM Finance Inc is a **Delaware** corporation.

For information on translations, please e-mail rights@apress.com, or visit http://www.apress.com/rights-permissions.

Apress titles may be purchased in bulk for academic, corporate, or promotional use. eBook versions and licenses are also available for most titles. For more information, reference our Print and eBook Bulk Sales web page at http://www.apress.com/bulk-sales.

Any source code or other supplementary material referenced by the author in this book is available to readers on GitHub via the book's product page, located at www.apress.com/978-1-4842-4400-5. For more detailed information, please visit http://www.apress.com/source-code.

Printed on acid-free paper

For my beloved mother and father.

Table of Contents

About the Author

Mohamed Mustapha Tahrioui has been a programmer for seven years and currently serves as a senior software engineer at axxessio. He is on the core team of the asyncio-heavy Telekom Smarthub project, where he offers his expertise for implementation, backward compatible architecture and implementation. He also offers full stack development via his IT consultancy Pi Intelligence, using Python, Java, JavaScript, Docker, PostgreSQL, MongoDB, and more.

About the Technical Reviewer

Said El Mallouki is a textbook computer geek with decades of experience designing and developing enterprise IT systems. His early encounters with the internals of computers took place at IBM's production facility in Germany more than two decades ago. In his current occupation as a technology lead, he is developing a toolchain for a natural language-understanding system at Deutsche Telekom. The intricacies of complex distributed systems were always on the top of his interest list. With three degrees in IT, business, and marketing, he combines a solid theoretical foundation with plenty of real-life experience. Living in Germany by the Rhine with his wife Andrea and their 18-month son Felix, his current favorite leisure activity is to be a devoted father.

Acknowledgments

I would like to express my deep gratitude to

> Mrs. Aditee Mirashi
> Mr. Todd Green
> Mr. Celestin Suresh John
> Mr. James Markham
> Mr. Matthew Moodle
> Mr. Said El Mallouki

for their invaluable efforts during the execution of my book.

Furthermore, my special thanks are extended to my company axxessio and in special to

> Mr. Goodarz Mahboobi
> Mr. Keyvan Mahbobi

Introduction

Motivation

The Python programming language adopted a preemptive concurrency framework in the early 90s via the threading module, which strived to mimic the Java concurrency library, as per the respective commit message.

A simple but powerful mechanism governs concurrent execution of bytecode in most Python implementations. This mechanism is called the *GIL* (global interpreter lock). The interpreter consumes one bytecode instruction at a time.

This effectively means that only one thread can run at the same time (in one interpreter process). Despite this fact, the underlying native thread implementation might be able to run more than one thread at a time.

The threads are appointed "fair" amounts of CPU time. Without employing sophisticated introspection techniques, this boils down to simple/naive time-based scheduling algorithms.

Taking this approach in the past would often yield inferior solutions to an equivalent single threaded program, for Python implementation with a GIL like CPython.

Since removing the GIL is not an option,[1] and prior attempts like Python safe-thread[2] failed because they degraded the single threading performance significantly, the concurrency situation meant having only the threading module.

---

[1] https://docs.python.org/3/faq/library.html#can-t-we-get-rid-of-the-global-interpreter-lock

[2] https://code.google.com/archive/p/python-safethread

What Is Asyncio?

The cooperative concurrency framework *asyncio* was written to address the need for fast single-threaded programs that don't waste CPU time on I/O bound tasks.

Its primitives like coroutines and event loops allow developers to execute code only when it's not waiting for I/O and to yield control back for other tasks.

Conclusion

Since its advent, asyncio has added countless APIs and keywords to the Python language (async/await). Its steep learning curve scares some developers from trying it. However, it's a powerful technology that's even been used by big players like Instagram[3].

The motivation of this book is to help more developers adopt asyncio and experience the joy of using asyncio for fun and profit. With that said, enjoy this book while learning more about asyncio!

---

[3]https://www.youtube.com/watch?v=ACgMTqX5Ee4

CHAPTER 1

Preparing for the Recipes

This chapter explains what asyncio is at a very high-level view and puts the APIs into perspective. It also explains the teaching approach that this book takes.

What Is Asyncio?

The Python language, in version 3.4, has adopted a powerful cooperative concurrency framework called *asyncio*. This cooperative concurrency framework can be roughly split into high- and low-level APIs, as shown in Figure 1-1.

© Mohamed Mustapha Tahrioui 2019
M. M. Tahrioui, *asyncio Recipes*, https://doi.org/10.1007/978-1-4842-4401-2_1

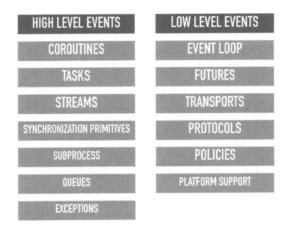

Figure 1-1. *High- and low-level APIs of asyncio*

A lot of usability improvements were added to asyncio in Python version 3.7, including the asyncio.run API, which abstracts direct access to event loops away and a couple of housekeeping tasks away from the developer.

As a result, the APIs for the most part are coroutines and task related. Nonetheless, more exotic APIs—like transports and protocols—are also discussed.

We feel that a bottom-up approach is better suited to teaching asyncio. Although We do classify some of these APIs as low-level, whereas they are often considered high-level. This approach is outlined in the next section.

What Is This Book's Approach to asyncio?

The book follows a bottom-up approach and can be roughly split into the topics shown in Figure 1-2.

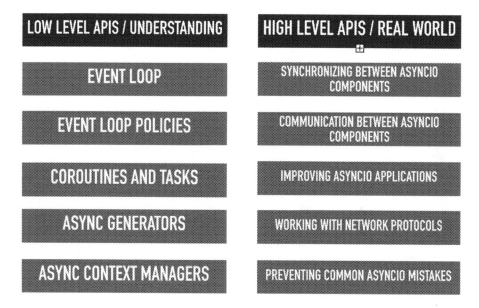

Figure 1-2. *The book's approach to asyncio*

The topics are roughly introduced in terms of:

- Importance: To get a firm understanding of asyncio

- Precedence: In case they are needed to explain more advanced topics

Since event loops live in the context of event loop policies—a concept singular to asyncio—the book's approach is to introduce low-level concepts like event loops, event loop policies, and watchers first. After that, we go over the coroutine and tasks APIs (which I consider low level too) that abstract the async working units.

Async generators and async context managers are powerful and compound, yet low-level tools and their respective use cases are discussed next.

In the high-level section, you learn how to:

- Make sure you do not run into race conditions when synchronizing, the Coffman conditions (necessary but not sufficient requirements for race conditions), asyncio's versions of locks and semaphores, and how race conditions manifest in asyncio code.

- Make asyncio components talk to each other, including how to implement traditional producer-consumer patterns, client-server schemes, etc.

- Improve an asyncio application, including how to migrate to a newer Python API version and how to detect deprecated APIs.

- Implement your own binary protocols and implement existing protocols, including how to use asyncio's powerful protocol and transport abstractions.

- Avoid common mistakes, including how to avoid too long-blocking code, miss an `await` keyword, etc.

This approach was chosen to support your journey toward understanding asyncio without too many technical intricacies at the wrong time. With that said, I hope you enjoy the book!

CHAPTER 2

Working with Event Loops

Python version 3.4 has adopted a powerful framework to support concurrent execution of code: asyncio. This framework uses event loops to orchestrate the callbacks and asynchronous tasks. Event loops live in the context of event loop policies—a concept singular to asyncio. The interplay among coroutines, event loops, and policies is illustrated in Figure 2-1.

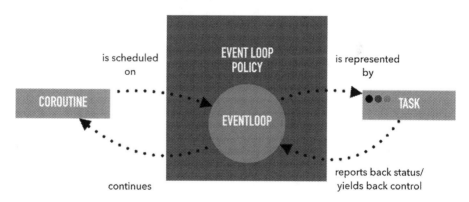

Figure 2-1. *Coroutines, event loops, and policies*

Coroutines can be thought of as functions you can "pause" at stages explicitly marked with some sort of syntactical element. The coroutine's state is tracked via a task object, instantiated by the respective event loop. The event loop keeps track of which task is currently running and delegates CPU time from idling coroutines to a pending one.

In the course of this chapter, we will find out more about the event loop's interface and its lifecycle. Event loop policies - and the impact global asyncio APIs have on them, will be discussed. For more information on the event loop concept, the different kinds of async work unit representations (callbacks, promises/futures, and coroutines), why event loops are OS specific, or guidance on subclassing an event loop, consult Appendix B.

Locating the Currently Running Loop

Problem

For various reasons, it is imperative that a concurrency framework is able to tell you whether an event loop is currently running and which one it is. For instance, it might be essential for your code to assert that only one certain loop implementation is running your task. Hence only one task can alter some shared resource or to be sure that your callbacks will be dispatched.

Solution

Use the global `asyncio.get_event_loop` and `asyncio.get_running_loop` APIs.

Option 1

```
import asyncio
loop = asyncio.get_event_loop()
```

Option 2

```
import asyncio
try:
    loop = asyncio.get_running_loop()

except RuntimeError:
    print("No loop running")
```

How It Works

In >= Python 3.7, there are two valid ways to get the currently running loop instance.

We can call asyncio.get_event_loop or asyncio.get_running_loop.

But what does asyncio.get_event_loop do under the hood? It is a convenience wrapper for the following:

1. Check if there is a loop running at the point of calling the function.

2. Return the running loop whose pid matches the current process pid, if there are any.

3. If not, get the thread-global LoopPolicy instance that's stored in a global variable in the asyncio module.

4. If it is not set, instantiate it with the DefaultLoopPolicy using a lock.

5. Note that the DefaultLoopPolicy is OS dependent and subclasses BaseDefaultEventLoopPolicy, which provides a default implementation of loop. get_event_loop, which is called.

6. Here is the catch: The loop_policy.get_event_loop
    method instantiates a loop only if you are on the
    main thread and assigns it to a thread local variable.

    If you are not on the main thread and no running
    loop is instantiated by other means, it will raise a
    RuntimeError.

This process has some issues:

- get_event_loop checks for the existence and returns
  the currently running loop.

- The event loop policy is stored thread globally, whereas
  the loop instance is stored thread locally.

- If you are on the main thread, get_event_loop will
  instantiate the loop and save the instance thread locally
  inside the policy.

- If you are not on the main thread, it will raise a
  RuntimeError.

asyncio.get_running_loop works differently. It will always return the
currently running loop instance if there is one running. If there is none, it
will raise a RuntimeError.

Creating a New Loop Instance
Problem

Since loops in asyncio are tightly coupled with the concept of loop
policies, it not advisable to create the loop instances via the loop
constructor. Otherwise, we might run into issues of scoping since the
global asyncio.get_event_loop function retrieves only loops that
either it created itself or was set via asyncio.set_event_loop.

Solution

To create a new event loop instance, we will use the `asyncio.new_event_loop` API.

Note   This API does not alter the currently installed event loop but initializes the (asyncio) global event loop policy - if it was not initialized before.

Another gotcha is that we will attach the newly created loop to the event loop policy's watcher to make sure that our event loop monitors the termination of newly spawned subprocesses on UNIX systems.

```python
import asyncio
import sys

loop = asyncio.new_event_loop()

print(loop) # Print the loop
asyncio.set_event_loop(loop)

if sys.platform != "win32":
    watcher = asyncio.get_child_watcher()
    watcher.attach_loop(loop)
```

How It Works

The `asyncio.get_event_loop` API only instantiates the loop if invoked from the main thread. Don't use any convenience wrappers to create the loop and store it yourself, like shown. This is sure to work on any thread and makes the creation of the loop side-effect free (besides the global creation of the `asyncio.DefaultLoopPolicy`).

Here is evidence that a loop is bound to a thread:

```
import asyncio
from threading import Thread

class LoopShowerThread(Thread):
    def run(self):
        try:
            loop = asyncio.get_event_loop()
            print(loop)
        except RuntimeError:
            print("No event loop!")

loop = asyncio.get_event_loop()
print(loop)

thread = LoopShowerThread()
thread.start()
thread.join()
```

In essence, this code contains a threading.Thread subclass definition that fetches the loop policy scoped loop.

Since we do not alter the DefaultLoopPolicy here, which holds one thread local loop, we can see that just calling asyncio.get_event_loop inside the LoopShowerThread is not enough to get a loop instance in a thread before instantiating it. The reason is that asyncio.get_event_loop simply creates a loop on the main thread.

Also, we can see that calling the following on the main thread beforehand does not affect the outcome, as predicted:

```
loop = asyncio.get_event_loop()
print(loop)
```

Attaching a Loop to the Thread Problem

Creating one loop per thread that's bond to the thread and which's finishing can be also awaited can be a challenging task. Later we learn about the executor API, which allows us to execute blocking coroutine calls as non-blocking calls by executing the respective calls on a thread pool.

Solution

Using the threading. Thread and the side-effect-free (besides event loop policy creation) asyncio.new_event_loop APIs, we can create thread instances that have unique event loop instances.

```python
import asyncio
import threading

def create_event_loop_thread(worker, *args, **kwargs):
    def _worker(*args, **kwargs):
        loop = asyncio.new_event_loop()
        asyncio.set_event_loop(loop)
      try:
            loop.run_until_complete(worker(*args, **kwargs))
        finally:
            loop.close()

    return threading.Thread(target=_worker, args=args,
    kwargs=kwargs)

async def print_coro(*args, **kwargs):
    print(f"Inside the print coro on {threading.get_ident()}:",
    (args, kwargs))

def start_threads(*threads):
    [t.start() for t in threads if isinstance(t, threading.Thread)]
```

```
def join_threads(*threads):
    [t.join() for t in threads if isinstance(t, threading.Thread)]

def main():
    workers = [create_event_loop_thread(print_coro) for i in
    range(10)]
    start_threads(*workers)
    join_threads(*workers)

if __name__ == '__main__':
    main()
```

How It Works

Loops live in the context of a loop policy. The DefaultLoopPolicy scopes
the loop per thread and does not allow creation of a loop outside a main
thread via asyncio.get_event_loop. Hence, we must create a thread local
event loop via asyncio.set_event_loop(asyncio.new_event_loop()).

We then await the asyncio.run_until_complete completion inside
our internal worker function called _worker by waiting for the thread to be
joined via join_threads.

Attaching a Loop to the Process

Problem

You have a multi-subprocess application that you want to asyncify.

Reasons for such a setup could be a primary-secondary setup, where
the primary process acts as the frontend to queries/requests and relays
them to multiple instances, which in turn use asyncio to use their CPU
time efficiently.

Solution #1 (UNIX Only)

We want to have process local event loops in a primary-secondary setup with event loops running in all processes (also the parent process).

For this matter, we share a dictionary across the processes that saves the event loop instances per process ID.

A helper function will contain the boilerplate to set up the event loop and save it per processes ID.

Note   The example is concise because of the UNIX-only APIs `os.register_at_fork` and `os.fork`. We do not have any error handling, which would be needed for a more sophisticated setup.

```python
import asyncio
import os

pid_loops = {}

def get_event_loop():
    return pid_loops[os.getpid()]

def asyncio_init():
    pid = os.getpid()
    if pid not in pid_loops:
        pid_loops[pid] = asyncio.new_event_loop()
        pid_loops[pid].pid = pid

if __name__ == '__main__':
    os.register_at_fork(after_in_parent=asyncio_init, after_in_
    child=asyncio_init)

    if os.fork() == 0:
        # Child
        loop = get_event_loop()
```

```
        pid = os.getpid()
        assert pid == loop.pid
        print(pid)
    else:
        # Parent
        loop = get_event_loop()
        pid = os.getpid()
        assert pid == loop.pid
        print(pid)
```

How It Works

The shown solution provides a way to have one event loop per process on a unix system and cache it inside the pid_loops dict. For creating a new process it uses the os.fork API which invokes the fork(2) system call. The fork(2) system call creates a new process by duplicating the old one. Since we call fork and then create the loops inside the parent and child process the pid_loops dict should be empty at the point after the os.fork call. Using the os.register_at_fork we register a hook which creates a new event loop instance and saving it to the pid_loops dict using the current pid as a key for the dict:

```
def asyncio_init():
    pid = os.getpid()
    if pid not in pid_loops:
        pid_loops[pid] = asyncio.new_event_loop()
        pid_loops[pid].pid = pid
```

This operation involves a pid lookup beforehand to ensure the event loop is only created and saved if there is none for the respective pid. This ensures that we create only one event loop per pid. We assert that this is true afterwards:

```
if os.fork() == 0:
    # Child
    loop = get_event_loop()
    pid = os.getpid()
    assert pid == loop.pid
    print(pid)
else:
    # Parent
    loop = get_event_loop()
    pid = os.getpid()
    assert pid == loop.pid
    print(pid)
```

Note   Using the return value of os.fork we can distinguish between the child and the parent process.

Solution #2

Using the more high-level multiprocessing module, we can build a cross-platform solution that runs multiple coroutines in process local event loops.

This way we can circumvent the CPython restrictions imposed by the GIL and leverage asyncio to improve our single core CPU usage on I/O intensive tasks.

```
import asyncio
import os
import random
import typing
from multiprocessing import Process

processes = []
```

```
def cleanup():
    global processes
    while processes:
        proc = processes.pop()
        try:
            proc.join()
        except KeyboardInterrupt:
            proc.terminate()

async def worker():
    random_delay = random.randint(0, 3)
    result = await asyncio.sleep(random_delay, result=f"Working
    in process: {os.getpid()}")
    print(result)

def process_main(coro_worker: typing.Callable, num_of_
coroutines: int, ):
    loop = asyncio.new_event_loop()
    try:
        workers = [coro_worker() for _ in range(num_of_coroutines)]
        loop.run_until_complete(asyncio.gather(*workers, loop=loop))
    except KeyboardInterrupt:
        print(f"Stopping {os.getpid()}")
        loop.stop()
    finally:
        loop.close()

def main(processes, num_procs, num_coros, process_main):
    for _ in range(num_procs):
        proc = Process(target=process_main, args=(worker, num_coros))
        processes.append(proc)
        proc.start()
```

```
if __name__ == '__main__':
    try:
        main(processes, 10, 2, process_main, )
    except KeyboardInterrupt:
        print("CTRL+C was pressed.. Stopping all subprocesses..")
    finally:
        cleanup()
        print("Cleanup finished")
```

How It Works

Using the multiprocessing package we can run subprocesses easily under all major distributions (Windows, Linux and Mac OS). This example illustrates how to write an application that uses the multiprocessing. Process class to run multiple coroutines in a separate Process. The function that will be run in each Process is the following:

```
def process_main(coro_worker: typing.Callable, num_of_
coroutines: int, ):
    loop = asyncio.new_event_loop()
    try:
        workers = [coro_worker() for _ in range(num_of_
        coroutines)]
        loop.run_until_complete(asyncio.gather(*workers,
        loop=loop))
    except KeyboardInterrupt:
        print(f"Stopping {os.getpid()}")
        loop.stop()
    finally:
        loop.close()
```

Note   You are advised to use `asyncio.run` instead of intantiating your own event loop. This example is only for illustrating how to instantiate event loops in different processes!

First we create a new event loop via `asyncio.new_event_loop`. Next we schedule some worker coroutines that simulate work via the `coro_worker` coroutine function:

```
async def worker():
    random_delay = random.randint(0, 3)
    result = await asyncio.sleep(random_delay, result=f"Working
    in process: {os.getpid()}")
    print(result)
```

We then schedule the workers using `asyncio.gather(*workers, loop=loop)` to benefit from asynchronous execution of the coroutines - if they yield back control back to the event loop via await `asyncio.sleep` (which they do).

The returned GatheringFuture instance is awaited via `loop.run_until_complete`. This ensures that the process terminates when all workers have returned.

In our parent process we schedule the processes via:

```
def main(processes, num_procs, num_coros, process_main):
    for _ in range(num_procs):
        proc = Process(target=process_main, args=(worker,
        num_coros))
        processes.append(proc)
        proc.start()
```

```
if __name__ == '__main__':
    try:
        main(processes, 10, 2, process_main, )
    except KeyboardInterrupt:
        print("CTRL+C was pressed.. Stopping all subprocesses..")
    finally:
        cleanup()
        print("Cleanup finished")
```

The main function creates the processes and appends them to the processes list. In the finally block we cleanup after the processes via:

```
def cleanup():
    global processes
    while processes:
        proc = processes.pop()
        try:
            proc.join()
        except KeyboardInterrupt:
            proc.terminate()
```

In the case we encounter a KeyboardInterrupt while we join we terminate the process via the process.terminate method.

Running a Loop
Problem

Callbacks and coroutines can only be scheduled on a running event loop per design. We need to know which loop API we need to invoke in order to transition the event loop state machine to the running state. We also need to identify the right area to schedule a callback/coroutine.

Solution

We learn which loop API we need to invoke in order to transition the event loop state machine to the running state and where the right place is to schedule a callback/coroutine.

```
import asyncio
import sys

loop = asyncio.new_event_loop()
asyncio.set_event_loop(loop)

if sys.platform != "win32":
    watcher = asyncio.get_child_watcher()
    watcher.attach_loop(loop)

# Use asyncio.ensure_future to schedule your first coroutines
# here or call loop.call_soon to schedule a synchronous callback

try:
    loop.run_forever()
finally:
    try:
        loop.run_until_complete(loop.shutdown_asyncgens())
    finally:
        loop.close()
```

How It Works

Calling `asyncio.new_event_loop` at the beginning of your script ensures that you have instantiated the global `DefaultLoopPolicy`.

The `loop_factory` of that loop policy is then invoked and the result - a new event loop, returned.

If we want to use the subprocess APIs of the loop, we need to attach the current child watcher by hand to ensure we can listen to the subprocess termination SIGCHLD signal. Since this is a UNIX API - meaning the SIGCHLD signal, we check if we are on a Windows system first.

Note   If we want to use subprocesses with event loops on Windows, we need to use the `ProactorEventLoop`, which we discuss in Chapter 9, "Working with Network Protocols".

Afterward, we invoke the `loop.run_forever` call. This call will block until we explicitly call `loop.stop` or an exception bubbles up.

Alternatively, we could use `loop.run_until_complete` to schedule one coroutine.

This also has the benefit that we do not have to call `loop.stop` explicitly. The loop runs until the coroutine passed to `loop.run_until_complete` is fully consumed.

Note that you can still call all the `loop.run_*` methods after calling `loop.stop`, whereas a `loop.close` will close the loop directly.

Running Async Code Without Bothering About Loops

Problem

Determine the most painless way to run a coroutine once, which might orchestrate all the other coroutines in your system.

Solution

1. Use the following code if you don't want to bother about tampering with loop policies and cleaning up after your asynchronous generators (you will learn about them in the next chapters). This is also good if you have only one thread and process and just one coroutine that needs to run from start to finish.

```
import asyncio

async def main():
    pass

asyncio.run(main())
```

How It Works

When you have a very simple setup and want to run a coroutine until it is completely awaited, you can use the `asyncio.run` API.

Note that it will call `asyncio.new_event_loop` and `asyncio.set_event_loop` for you and is hence not side-effect free.

Note   The `asyncio.run` API cancels the remaining tasks in a *non-threadsafe* fashion (it doesn't use `loop.call_soon_threadsafe` to cancel the tasks) and has an optional debug parameter that is passed to the loop.

This API will also invoke the async generator cleanup hook called `loop.shutdown_asyncgens` on the loop.

Note   This is the recommended way to run simple and/or single-threaded asyncio applications.

Running a Loop Until a Coroutine Finishes
Problem

Running a coroutine until the coroutine finishes is one of the most basic yet most important tasks a loop must be able to do. Without this capability, loops are pretty much useless. This is because you would have no indication whatsoever that your workload was consumed, hence leaving you without leeway for making assumptions in the code.

Solution #1

Given that we want to couple the coroutine's lifetime with the loop, we can use two methods. We can allocate a loop and schedule the coroutine on the loop (and have to deal with all the cleanup actions ourselves) or use more high-level APIs like `asyncio.run`.

```
import asyncio

async def main():
    pass

asyncio.run(main())
```

How It Works

Basically, we can reuse the setup from the last answer to run a coroutine until it was consumed. The same rules apply here.

asyncio.run takes care of the cleanup and stops the event loop.

Note   asyncio.run works very well with simple setups in conjunction with the asyncio.get_running_loop() API.

Solution #2

In settings in which asyncio.run is not available, you can invoke asyncio. get_event_loop or asyncio.new_event_loop yourself. We will look at the first case:

```
import asyncio

async def main():
    pass

loop = asyncio.get_event_loop()

try:
    loop.run_until_complete(main())
finally:
    try:
        loop.run_until_complete(loop.shutdown_asyncgens())
    finally:
        loop.close()
```

How It Works

This generates the loop in the same fashion as Solution #1, with the exception that it will generate a loop only if we are on the main thread. It will otherwise raise a RuntimeError.

We have to call `loop.shutdown_asyncgens` ourselves to clean up after any not completely consumed async generators. (We learn about async generators in Chapter 6, "Communication Between Asyncio Components".)

Solution #3

The `asyncio.new_event_loop` API is the lowest-level asyncio API that creates a new event loop instance while respecting the currently installed event loop policy.

Using it involves a lot of manual work, like attaching the loop to the current child watcher or cleaning up the async generators.

Be aware that might be necessary in more complex setups that span multiple processes or to better understand what happens behind the scenes of asyncio.

```python
import asyncio
import sys

async def main():
    pass

loop = asyncio.new_event_loop()
asyncio.set_event_loop(loop)

if sys.platform != "win32":
    watcher = asyncio.get_child_watcher()
    watcher.attach_loop(loop)
try:
    loop.run_forever()
finally:
    try:
        loop.run_until_complete(loop.shutdown_asyncgens())
    finally:
        loop.close()
```

How It Works

It works the same as Solution #2 does, but you can call it from a thread. The reason for this is because we do not use the convenience API `asyncio. get_event_loop`, which performs a main thread equality check.

Note   This is similar to what the `asyncio.run` API does under the hood.

Scheduling Callbacks on a Loop

Problem

Event loops can be used in a callback-oriented fashion or with coroutines.

The latter is considered the superior pattern in asyncio but for use cases like timers or for timing-based state machines, a callback API with delayable callbacks can yield very elegant and concise results.

Solution #1

We will learn about the `loop.call_*` APIs, which can be used to schedule synchronous callbacks on the event loop.

```
import asyncio

loop = asyncio.get_event_loop()
loop.call_soon(print, "I am scheduled on a loop!")
loop.call_soon_threadsafe(print, "I am scheduled on a loop but
threadsafely!")
loop.call_later(1, print, "I am scheduled on a loop in one second")
loop.call_at(loop.time() + 1, print, "I am scheduled on a loop in
one second too")
```

```
try:
    print("Stop the loop by hitting the CTRL+C keys...")
    # To see the callbacks running you need to start the running loop
    loop.run_forever()
except KeyboardInterrupt:
    loop.stop()
finally:
    loop.close()
```

How It Works

For calling functions on the event loop, we have four methods at our disposal:

- `call_soon`
- `call_soon_threadsafe`
- `call_at`
- `call_later`

None of the `loop.call_*` methods is thread-safe except for `loop.call_soon_threadsafe`.

All these methods support the new keyword-only parameter, `context`. The `context` parameter needs to be an instance of Context, which is an API introduced by PEP 567. The rationale of this parameter is to provide means to "manage, store, and access context-local state".

All the changes made by the `loop.call_*` methods to any context variable are preserved in it. The callback methods don't provide a way to cleanly wait for them to be consumed.

This is why we employ the `KeyboardInterrupt` pattern. We need to signal our process with the Ctrl+C key to stop the loop. We learn about a cleaner alternative in the next solution.

Solution #2

Unfortunately, asyncio does not provide a nice API to await these scheduled callbacks. The handles returned by the APIs can also only be used to cancel pending callbacks.

There is a way to manipulate the event loop to make these callbacks awaitable.

```
import asyncio
from functools import partial as func

class SchedulerLoop(asyncio.SelectorEventLoop):
    def __init__(self):
        super(SchedulerLoop, self).__init__()
        self._scheduled_callback_futures = []

    @staticmethod
    def unwrapper(fut: asyncio.Future, function):
        """

        Function to get rid of the implicit fut parameter.
        :param fut:
        :type fut:
        :param function:
        :return:
        """

        return function()

    def _future(self, done_hook):
        """

        Create a future object that calls the done_hook when it
        is awaited
        :param loop:
        :param function:
        :return:
        """
```

```python
    fut = self.create_future()
    fut.add_done_callback(func(self.unwrapper,
    function=done_hook))
    return fut

def schedule_soon_threadsafe(self, callback, *args,
context=None):
    fut = self._future(func(callback, *args))
    self._scheduled_callback_futures.append(fut)
    self.call_soon_threadsafe(fut.set_result, None,
    context=context)

def schedule_soon(self, callback, *args, context=None):
    fut = self._future(func(callback, *args))
    self._scheduled_callback_futures.append(fut)
    self.call_soon(fut.set_result, None, context=context)

def schedule_later(self, delay_in_seconds, callback, *args,
context=None):
    fut = self._future(func(callback, *args))
    self._scheduled_callback_futures.append(fut)
    self.call_later(delay_in_seconds, fut.set_result, None,
    context=context)
def schedule_at(self, delay_in_seconds, callback, *args,
context=None):
    fut = self._future(func(callback, *args))
    self._scheduled_callback_futures.append(fut)
    self.call_at(delay_in_seconds, fut.set_result, None,
    context=context)

async def await_callbacks(self):
    callback_futs = self._scheduled_callback_futures[:]
    self._scheduled_callback_futures[:] = []
    await asyncio.gather(*callback_futs)
```

```
async def main(loop):
    loop.schedule_soon_threadsafe(print, "hallo")
    loop.schedule_soon(print, "This will be printed when the
    loop starts running")

    def callback(value):
        print(value)

    loop.schedule_soon_threadsafe(func(callback, value="This
    will get printed when the loop starts running"))
    offset_in_seconds = 4
    loop.schedule_at(loop.time() + offset_in_seconds,
                     func(print, f"This will be printed after
                     {offset_in_seconds} seconds"))
    loop.schedule_later(offset_in_seconds, func(print, f"This
    will be printed after {offset_in_seconds} seconds too"))
    await loop.await_callbacks()

loop = SchedulerLoop()
loop.run_until_complete(main(loop))
```

How It Works

Since we don't have a clean API to wait for scheduled synchronous
callbacks via await, we create one.

The gist is that we can provide our own loop implementation based on
SelectorEventLoop and thin wrapper methods around the loop.call_*
methods that save a future that we can wait on.

The future is lazy consumed since the callbacks are set with future.
add_done_callback.

When you await the future, the point of consumption is the asyncio.
gather call in the coroutine method await_callbacks.

Basically every time we invoke a `loop.call_*` call, we save a future to the `loop._scheduled_callback_futures` property.

Scheduling Coroutines on a Loop

Problem

We have learned how to schedule callbacks on a loop. The preferred way in asyncio, however, is to use coroutines. They involve the least amount of boilerplate code and are easier to reason about than asynchronous code built around callbacks.

Solution #1

Option 1

If there is no running event loop, we can use `asyncio.ensure_future` in conjunction with `asyncio.run`:

```python
import asyncio
import random

async def work(i):
    print(await asyncio.sleep(random.randint(0, i),
    result=f"Concurrent work {i}"))

async def main():
    tasks = [asyncio.ensure_future(work(i)) for i in range(10)]
    await asyncio.gather(*tasks)

asyncio.run(main())
```

Option 2

If we do not want to write a `main` coroutine, we can use `loop.run_until_complete` instead:

```
import asyncio
import random

async def work(i):
    print(await asyncio.sleep(random.randint(0, i),
    result=f"Concurrent work {i}"))

loop = asyncio.get_event_loop()
tasks = [asyncio.ensure_future(work(i)) for i in range(10)]

loop.run_until_complete(asyncio.gather(*tasks))
```

How It Works

To schedule coroutines on loops, we can use four mechanisms:

- The `await` keyword
- The `loop.create_task` method
- The `asyncio.ensure_future`
- The `asyncio.create_task`

We can use the `await` keyword which blocks until the coroutine either returns or uses the `asyncio.sleep` await to yield back control over the execution flow. The await keyword can be used in coroutine functions only.

The `loop.create_task` method schedules the coroutine and immediately returns a task object that can be used to wait for the coroutine to finish. It can be used in synchronous contexts and coroutine functions. The only disadvantage is that it's fairly low-level, and we need a loop instance to invoke it.

Next up is the `asyncio.ensure_future` API, which can also be called in both coroutine functions and synchronous contexts. It consumes both tasks and coroutines. If there is no loop running, it will schedule it on the loop stored in the default loop event policy by fetching it via `asyncio.get_event_loop` and then calling `loop.create_task`.

Note the coroutines/tasks will run once the loop is actually running and that you cannot schedule the same task on two loops with this API.

`asyncio.create_task` is the preferred way to schedule coroutines on an event loop.

`asyncio.create_task` will raise a runtime error if no loop is running, so essentially it can be used with coroutine functions or callbacks that are scheduled on the loop via `loop.call_*` - because such a handler can only be called by a running event loop.

In this example we can use two mechanisms here—`await` and `asyncio.ensure_future`.

Inside the coroutine, we await on `asyncio.sleep` with a random sleep delay to simulate work. The `result` keyword-only parameter returns a value after the sleep delay.

Since using `asyncio.ensure_future` like that means that our coroutines are now scheduled, we find ourselves in a situation where we need to wait for the execution to finish.

To wait for all of the pending tasks, we wrap them into an `asyncio.gather` call and await the resulting `GatheringFuture` by calling `loop.run_until_complete` or awaiting it inside a coroutine that can be scheduled via `asyncio.run`.

Solution #2

Using our knowledge about event loops and event loop policies, we can write our own loop implementation that provides an API to cleanly wait for all pending coroutines.

This can be helpful when asyncio.all_tasks() returns too many tasks for a given event loop and waiting for a subset of tasks is sufficient.

```python
import asyncio

async def work():
    print("Main was called.")

class AsyncSchedulerLoop(asyncio.SelectorEventLoop):

    def __init__(self):
        super(AsyncSchedulerLoop, self).__init__()
        self.coros = asyncio.Queue(loop=self)

    def schedule(self, coro):
        task = self.create_task(coro)
        task.add_done_callback(lambda _: self.coros.task_done())
        self.coros.put_nowait(task)

    async def wait_for_all(self):
        await self.coros.join()

class AsyncSchedulerLoopPolicy(asyncio.DefaultEventLoopPolicy):
    def new_event_loop(self):
        return AsyncSchedulerLoop()

asyncio.set_event_loop_policy(AsyncSchedulerLoopPolicy())
loop = asyncio.get_event_loop()

for i in range(1000):
    loop.schedule(work())

loop.run_until_complete(loop.wait_for_all())
```

How It Works

If we want to make sure that we just await the tasks that we have scheduled by means of the loop.create_task method, we can do so by writing our own loop implementation.

We use an asyncio queue to hold the tasks for convenience.

Note that this implies that we consume tasks in a FIFO (first in, first out) fashion, which corresponds to how loop.call_* methods are consumed.

Why do we use a queue? Because we get the part for free where we wait for all tasks to finish: we just have to await the queue's queue.join coroutine!

We can use the queue's queue.task_done method to signal we have consumed a coroutine, but at what point? A good place to do so is in the done_callback of the task—where we ultimately end up calling it.

Calling Blocking Code on a Loop

Problem

Only one callback can run on an asyncio event loop at a time. Hence, a long running callback may block the event loop for others if it is executing for too long. Event loops expose an executor API that addresses this issue. We will learn about the executor API in the following example.

Solution

We use urllib3 as a blocking HTTP client library, which we will asyncify. Hence, you need to install the certifi and urllib3 packages via the package manager of your choice. For example, via pip or pipenv:

```
pip3 install urllib3==1.23
pip3 install certifi==2018.04.16
```

```
# or
pipenv install urllib3==1.23
pipenv install certifi==2018.04.16
```

Note   In this example, we use `certifi` for collections of root certificates, which we can use to query TLS-secured websites over HTTPS.

```
import asyncio
from concurrent.futures.thread
import ThreadPoolExecutor
import certifi
import urllib3

HTTP_POOL_MANAGER = urllib3.PoolManager(ca_certs=certifi.where())
EXECUTOR = ThreadPoolExecutor(10)
URL = https://apress.com

async def block_request(http, url, *, executor=None, loop:
asyncio.AbstractEventLoop):
    return await loop.run_in_executor(executor, http.request,
    "GET", url)

def multi_block_requests(http, url, n, *, executor=None, loop:
asyncio.AbstractEventLoop):
    return (asyncio.ensure_future(block_request(http, url,
    executor=executor, loop=loop)) for _ in range(n))

async def consume_responses(*coro, loop):
    result = await asyncio.gather(*coro, loop=loop, return_
    exceptions=True)
```

```
for res in result:
    if not isinstance(res, Exception):
        print(res.data)
loop = asyncio.get_event_loop()
loop.set_default_executor(EXECUTOR)
loop.run_until_complete(consume_responses(block_request(HTTP_
POOL_MANAGER, URL, loop=loop),loop=loop))
loop.run_until_complete(
    consume_responses(*multi_block_requests(HTTP_POOL_MANAGER,
    URL, 10, loop=loop), loop=loop))
```

How It Works

To call a blocking function with asyncio, we can use the loop.run_in_
executor coroutine method. It will return an awaitable that, if awaited,
returns a future with the result of the blocking call. This means loop.run_
in_executor is lazy evaluated by definition.

How does it work under the hood? Basically an executor (like a
ThreadPoolExecutor) is used to schedule a blocking synchronous call
while also asyncifying it. In the case of the ThreadPoolExecutor, thread
preemption is used to provide the non-blocking experience. Note that the
CPython implementation has a global mutex object called the GIL, which
decreases the effectiveness of native p-threads.

Note   It is discouraged to use ProcessPoolExecutor. In fact,
it will be prohibited via set_default_executor in Python 3.8.
Source: https://bugs.python.org/issue34075.

Here is an example of asyncifying the `urllib3.PoolManager`. Its request method is scheduled on the executor:

```
return await loop.run_in_executor(executor, http.request,
"GET", url).
```

Using a `asyncio.gather` call and a generator expression, we can schedule multiple requests at the same time. That part is provided by `consume_responses` which silences exceptions too.

Running a Coroutine Specifically on One Loop

Problem

To make sure that you run your coroutine specifically on one loop, you have two methods, as explained next.

Solution #1

Getting an event loop instance and running a coroutine on it ensures that the coroutine runs on specifically that loop. To ensure that the same loop is used in chained coroutines, the `asyncio.get_running_loop` is used:

```
import asyncio

async def main(loop):
    assert loop == asyncio.get_running_loop()

loop = asyncio.get_event_loop()
loop.run_until_complete(main(loop))
```

How It Works

If the loop is not running, the easiest way to run it is to schedule the coroutine on the loop via `loop.run_until_complete`.

If the coroutine is a built-in with a keyword-only loop parameter, pass it.

Note   Passing a loop explicitly via the keyword-only loop parameter is considered deprecated, which we discuss in Chapter 8, "Improving Asyncio Applications".

Solution #2

By using the `loop.create_task` API, it is ensured that a coroutine will run on a specific loop.

To use it, an event loop instance must be acquired:

```python
import asyncio

async def main():
    pass

loop = asyncio.get_event_loop()
task = loop.create_task(main())
task.add_done_callback(lambda fut: loop.stop())
# Or more generic if you don't have loop in scope:
# task.add_done_callback(lambda fut: asyncio.get_running_
loop().stop())

loop.run_forever()
```

How It Works

If the loop is already running, we use the `asyncio.ensure_future` method to schedule a coroutine on the loop.

Note   If you are inside a coroutine, use `asyncio.create_task` instead!

The same observations from Solution #1 apply, with the additional notice that we need to explicitly stop the loop in this case.

Stopping and Closing a Loop

Problem

As we learned earlier, the event loop has an internal state machine that indicates which of its lifecycle duties are to be executed. For instance, only a running event loop may schedule new callbacks. An event loop that is in the running state will continue to run indefinitely if it's not halted properly.

Solution

In this section, we learn when and how to stop an event loop. We can do so via the stop/close APIs.

```python
import asyncio
import functools

async def main(loop):
    print("Print in main")

def stop_loop(fut, *, loop):
    loop.call_soon_threadsafe(loop.stop)
```

```
loop = asyncio.get_event_loop()
tasks = [loop.create_task(main(loop)) for _ in range(10)]
asyncio.gather(*tasks).add_done_callback(functools.
partial(stop_loop, loop=loop))
try:
    loop.run_forever()
finally:
    try:
        loop.run_until_complete(loop.shutdown_asyncgens())
    finally:
        loop.close()# optional
```

How It Works

What happens here is that we have a loop instance that we run via `loop.run_forever`.

We have scheduled a couple of tasks and saved them in a list. To be able to stop our loop properly, we need to make sure we have consumed all of the tasks, so we wrap them with a call to `asyncio.gather` and add a `done_callback` to it, which closes our loop.

This ensures we have finished our work when we close the loop.

Note that we also call `loop.shutdown_asyncgens`, which should become second habit when you close a loop. We explain this in further detail in Chapter 4, "Generators".

Adding a Loop Signal Handler

Problem

You need to use signal handlers with loops. We need a setup that runs the signal handlers only when our loop is running and that disallows new signal handlers when the loop is not running.

41

Solution (UNIX Only)

Ideally, the event loop should clean up the signal handlers. Fortunately, asyncio provides such APIs out of the box.

```python
import asyncio
import functools
import os
import signal

SIGNAL_NAMES = ('SIGINT', 'SIGTERM')
SIGNAL_NAME_MESSAGE = " or ".join(SIGNAL_NAMES)

def sigint_handler(signame, *, loop, ):
    print(f"Stopped loop because of {signame}")
    loop.stop()

def sigterm_handler(signame, *, loop, ):
    print(f"Stopped loop because of {signame}")
    loop.stop()

loop = asyncio.get_event_loop()

for signame in SIGNAL_NAMES:
    loop.add_signal_handler(getattr(signal, signame),
                            functools.partial(locals()
[f"{signame.lower()}_handler"], signame, loop=loop))
print("Event loop running forever, press Ctrl+C to interrupt.")
print(f"pid {os.getpid()}: send {SIGNAL_NAME_MESSAGE} to
exit.")
try:
    loop.run_forever()
finally:
    loop.close() # optional
```

How It Works

Basically, we add a new `signal_handler` via `loop.add_signal_handler`. It is analogous to the signal API. In this case, we decided to stop the loop at the end of every handler. We provide it via `functools.partial` and take the handler that is in scope via the `locales` built-in.

If you want to add another handler to the example, you just add the name of the signal to `SIGNAL_NAMES` and a corresponding handler named in this fashion:

```
"{signame.lower()}_handler"
```

Why not use the signal API directly? The signal handlers you add to the loop are checked in the course of a loop iteration. Hence, it is not possible to add a signal handler to the loop when it is closed.

Another perk is that the signal handlers are cleaned up for you when the loop closes.

Spawning a Subprocess from a Loop

Problem

Asynchronously spawning a subprocess and effectively splitting creation and state management in separate parts is one of the reasons to use a loop to spawn a subprocess.

Solution

The following solution is sufficient for most non-interactive uses of the asyncio subprocess APIs. It has the benefit of being cross-platform by setting the appropriate event loop policy on a Windows system.

```
import asyncio
import shutil
```

43

```
import sys
from typing import Tuple, Union

async def invoke_command_async(*command, loop,
encoding="UTF-8", decode=True) -> Tuple[
    Union[str, bytes], Union[str, bytes], int]:
    """

    Invoke a command asynchronously and return the stdout,
    stderr and the process return code.
    :param command:
    :param loop:
    :param encoding:
    :param decode:
    :return:
    """

    if sys.platform != 'win32':
        asyncio.get_child_watcher().attach_loop(loop)
    process = await asyncio.create_subprocess_exec(*command,
                                            stdout=asyncio.
                                            subprocess.PIPE,
                                            stderr=asyncio.
                                            subprocess.PIPE,
                                            loop=loop)

    out, err = await process.communicate()

    ret_code = process.returncode

    if not decode:
        return out, err, ret_code

    output_decoded, err_decoded = out.decode(encoding) if out
                                  else None,
                                  err.decode(encoding) if err
                                  else None
```

```
    return output_decoded, err_decoded, ret_code

async def main(loop):
    out, err, retcode = await invoke_command_async(shutil.
    which("ping"), "-c", "1", "8.8.8.8", loop=loop)
    print(out, err, retcode)

if sys.platform == "win32":
    asyncio.set_event_loop_policy(asyncio.
    WindowsProactorEventLoopPolicy())

loop = asyncio.get_event_loop()
loop.run_until_complete(main(loop))
```

How It Works

To properly spawn a subprocess from a loop, we introduce an asynchronous helper called invoke_command_async.

This helper coroutine function uses the loop's create_subprocess_exec method to create a subprocess.

Under UNIX, we have a class in asyncio called AbstractChildWatcher, whose implementation is used to watch the termination of subprocesses.

To properly work, the ChildWatcher needs to be attached to an event loop. When you have one loop instance, this might be fine, but when you create your loops via asyncio.new_event_loop, etc., you need to make sure the current loop policy's ChildWatcher is attached to it. You can do so by calling the watcher's watcher.attach_loop method, as shown here:

```
if sys.platform != 'win32':
        asyncio.get_child_watcher().attach_loop(loop)
```

The next part is lazily (by means of a future) getting the process instance via create_subprocess_exec.

The API for the process instance is analogue to the synchronous one. You need to await the coroutine methods like process.communicate. In theory, this gives you the flexibility to await it another time, but it's not necessary for the sake of this example.

Waiting for Subprocess Termination

Problem

The goal here is to watch a subprocess terminate hassle-free even under Windows, which does not have a full signal API and hence does not support SIGCHLD.

Solution

To ensure that we can await the termination of our subprocesses under Windows, we will poll the subprocesses for a process return code, which indicates a terminated subprocess.

```
import asyncio

# Quote from https://docs.python.org/3/library/asyncio-
subprocess.html:
# The child watcher must be instantiated in the main thread,
before executing subprocesses from other threads. Call the get_
child_watcher() function in the main thread to instantiate the
child watcher.
import functools
import shutil
import sys
```

```python
if sys.platform == "win32":
    asyncio.set_event_loop_policy(asyncio.
WindowsProactorEventLoopPolicy())

def stop_loop(*args, loop, **kwargs):
    loop.stop()

async def is_windows_process_alive(process, delay=0.5):
    """

    On windows the signal API is very sparse, meaning we don't
    have SIGCHLD. So we just check if we have a return code on
    our process object.
    :param process:
    :param delay:
    :return:
    """

    while process.returncode == None:
        await asyncio.sleep(delay)

async def main(process_coro, *, loop):
    process = await process_coro
    if sys.platform != "win32":
        child_watcher: asyncio.AbstractChildWatcher = asyncio.
        get_child_watcher()
        child_watcher.add_child_handler(process.pid, functools.
        partial(stop_loop, loop=loop))
    else:
        await is_windows_process_alive(process)
        loop.stop()

loop = asyncio.get_event_loop()
```

```
process_coro = asyncio.create_subprocess_exec(shutil.
                                              which("ping"),
                                              "-c", "1",
                                              "127.0.0.1",
                                              stdout=asyncio.
                                              subprocess.
                                              DEVNULL,
                                              stderr=asyncio.
                                              subprocess.
                                              DEVNULL)

loop.create_task(main(process_coro, loop=loop))
loop.run_forever()
```

How It Works

For UNIX systems, it is quite easy to detect when a subprocess terminates because the process changes its state and announces this via SIGCHLD. Coupled with the waitpid(2) syscall, which can detect process state changes and blocks, we have a powerful tool to react to process termination without the cost of a busy loop.

On Windows, it is not that easy. The signaling API is very limited and just exposes SIGTERM and SIGINT. Hence, we must poll the process return code which is set on process termination, because Windows only uses this POSIX standard.

On Windows we do so via is_windows_process_alive. In Unix, we could just use invoke_command_async, instead of attaching a child handler to the watcher, which does basically the same thing. The watcher gets attached to the loop and conveniently calls watcher.add_child_handler for us.

CHAPTER 3

Working with Coroutines and Async/Await

A *coroutine* is a work unit for an event loop/scheduler and can be understood as a suspendible function. The "co" in coroutine does not stem from the word concurrent, but rather from the word *cooperative*.

The coroutine "cooperates" with the event loop that schedules the coroutine. If the coroutine is "logically blocked," meaning it waits on some sort of I/O, the coroutine can yield control back to the event loop. The loop can then decide how to use the freed resources (CPU time) to dispatch other "waiting and ready" coroutines. The loop can then decide how to use the freed resources (CPU time) to dispatch other pending coroutines.

In asyncio, we differentiate between a *coroutine* and a *coroutine function*. The coroutine is the object returned by the coroutine function and can be in a running, finished, cancelled, or suspended state. We use the terms interchangeably if doing so doesn't cause ambiguity.

© Mohamed Mustapha Tahrioui 2019
M. M. Tahrioui, *asyncio Recipes*, https://doi.org/10.1007/978-1-4842-4401-2_3

Writing Generator-Based Coroutine Functions

Problem

We cannot use coroutines defined with the async keyword in a pre-3.5 Python interpreter.

Solution

Functions that are defined with the @asyncio.coroutine decorator are called *generator-based* and they provide the means to write a coroutine in a pre-3.5 Python interpreter.

```
import asyncio

@asyncio.coroutine
def coro():
    value = yield from inner()
    print(value)

@asyncio.coroutine
def inner():
    return [1, 2, 3]

asyncio.run(coro()) # will print [1, 2, 3]
```

How It Works

The @asyncio.coroutine decorator can be used to write generator-based coroutines.

In their bodies we can only use the yield from keyword to call other coroutines or suspend them—using await will raise a SyntaxError.

However, using `yield from` on a native coroutine object, like `asyncio.sleep(1)`, in a non-coroutine generator will raise a `TypeError`:

```
import asyncio

def main():
  yield from asyncio.sleep(1)

asyncio.run(main())
```

Note   Generator-based coroutines have been deprecated since Python version 3.7 and will be removed in Python version 3.10.

Also note that the decorator is not strictly enforced. This means we can run functions with `yield from` inside their bodies on the event loop too!

Writing a Native Coroutine

Problem

Being able to write a coroutine is the first step to using `asyncio` in a productive fashion.

Solution

Native coroutine functions are functions that return a coroutine, which in turn is a cooperatively scheduled asyncio primitive. They are the preferred way to write a coroutine function. Native coroutine functions are defined with the `async def` syntax.

They are equivalent to the deprecated generator-based coroutine functions in respect to their function and return native coroutine objects.

The async def transports all the semantics needed to define a coroutine function. There is no need to include an await keyword inside the coroutine function body.

```
import asyncio

async def coroutine(*args, **kwargs):
    pass

assert asyncio.iscoroutine(coroutine())
assert asyncio.iscoroutinefunction(coroutine)
```

How It Works

Given that you have a coroutine function with the async keyword, you can use the await keyword in its body to await other coroutines.

Using the predicate functions inspect.iscoroutine and inspect. iscoroutinefunction, we can determine if an object is in fact a native coroutine (function).

The coroutines run on the loop implementations provided by asyncio and delegate to other coroutines only with the await keyword.

Note   Every time you could have used yield from in a generator-based coroutine, you now have to use the await keyword inside the coroutine function body.

Running a Coroutine and Blocking/Waiting Until It Finishes

Problem

A syntactic mechanism is needed to pinpoint the moment when a coroutine finishes. This mechanism must also be suspendable and resumable.

Solution

Using the await keyword, we are equipped to handle awaiting native coroutines in the intended fashion.

```
import asyncio

async def coroutine(*args,**kwargs):
    print("Waiting for the next coroutine...")
    await another_coroutine(*args,**kwargs)
    print("This will follow 'Done'")

async def another_coroutine(*args,**kwargs):
    await asyncio.sleep(3)
    print("Done")
```

How It Works

The coroutine function called coroutine has a statement called await another_coroutine(*args,**kwargs) in its body that uses the await keyword to signal to the event loop that it awaits the completion of another_coroutine.

The same mechanism is used in the await asyncio.sleep(3) statement to halt the execution of the containing coroutine.

Basically, an await is a `yield from` with an additional awaitable type check and more intuitive operator precedencies, which are reflected in the following table:

Operator	Description
`yield x, yield from x`	Yield expression
`lambda`	Lambda expression
`if -- else`	Conditional expression
`or`	Boolean OR
`and`	Boolean AND
`not x`	Boolean NOT
`in, not in, is, is not, <, <=, >,` `>=, !=, ==`	Comparisons, including membership tests and identity tests
`|`	Bitwise OR
`^`	Bitwise XOR
`&`	Bitwise AND
`<<, >>`	Shifts
`+, -`	Addition and subtraction
`*, @, /, //, %`	Multiplication, matrix multiplication, division, remainder
`+x, -x, ~x`	Positive, negative, bitwise NOT
`**`	Exponentiation
`await x`	Await expression
`x[index], x[index:index],` `x(arguments...),x.attribute`	Subscription, slicing, call, attribute reference
`(expressions...), [expressions...],` `{key:value...}, {expressions...}`	Binding or tuple display, list display, dictionary display, set display

The updates precedencies make constructs like `return await` possible. Previously, you had to put `yield from` and the following coroutine into parentheses to do this:

```
return (yield from asyncio.sleep(1))

# vs.

return await asyncio.sleep(1)
```

Running a Coroutine and Waiting for It to Finish

Problem

We have learned how to block until a coroutine has finished executing. But we want to defer the waiting to a certain place to decouple scheduling the coroutine. We also want to be able to pinpoint when it is finished and to schedule callbacks at that time.

Solution

Using the `await` keyword in conjunction with `asyncio.create_task`, we can decouple running a coroutine from awaiting it.

```
import asyncio

async def coroutine_to_run():
    print(await asyncio.sleep(1, result="I have finished!"))

async def main():
    task = asyncio.create_task(coroutine_to_run())
    await task

asyncio.run(main())
```

How It Works

This solution is very similar to the previous one. It schedules the coroutine `coroutine_to_run` using `asyncio.create_task` and returns a task that can be used to await said scheduled coroutine.

Note   The coroutine starts running shortly after the call to `asyncio.create_task`.

Since splitting up the scheduling of the task and awaiting it, we have the flexibility to create code that has sequence assurances while also being able to schedule more work or attach callbacks to be executed on consumption.

Note   Using callbacks is discouraged since the order in which the callbacks are dispatched is undefined and an implementation detail.

Waiting on a Coroutine with a Timeout

Problem

Given a coroutine that needs to be scheduled and a timeout in seconds, how do we cancel a scheduled routine if it doesn't complete in that timeframe?

Solution

Ideally, we don't want to schedule another coroutine to cancel a routine. It would be better to specify this on "scheduling time".

```python
import asyncio

async def delayed_print(text, delay):
    print(await asyncio.sleep(delay, text))

async def main():
    delay = 3

    on_time_coro = delayed_print(f"I will print after {delay}
    seconds", delay)
    await  asyncio.wait_for(on_time_coro, delay + 1)

    try:
        delayed_coro = delayed_print(f"I will print after
        {delay+1} seconds", delay + 1)
        await  asyncio.wait_for(delayed_coro, delay)
    except asyncio.TimeoutError:
        print(f"I timed out after {delay} seconds")

asyncio.run(main())
```

How It Works

As we can see, asyncio provides the `asyncio.wait_for` function.

It safely returns from a call given a coroutine that runs in the time boundaries or otherwise throws an `asyncio.TimeoutError`.

Cancelling a Coroutine

Problem

Designing a sophisticated concurrent system might require the need to cancel the workloads you have scheduled on the event loop.

Think about this execution scenario: You want to send a personalized email to a database of customers. The personalization requires a web query and sending out the email requires a database query.

These queries can run concurrently. If either of them results in an error, the other query will need to be cancelled.

We will learn how to cancel a scheduled coroutine thread-safely and not thread-safely.

Solution #1

Using the task object we receive from `asyncio.create_task`, it is possible to control the execution state of the underlying coroutine.

```python
import asyncio

async def cancellable(delay=10):
    loop = asyncio.get_running_loop()
    try:
        now = loop.time()
        print(f"Sleeping from {now} for {delay} seconds ...")
        await asyncio.sleep(delay, loop=loop)
        print(f"Slept {delay} seconds ...")
    except asyncio.CancelledError:
        print(f"Cancelled at {now} after {loop.time()-now}
        seconds")

async def main():
    coro = cancellable()
    task = asyncio.create_task(coro)
    await asyncio.sleep(3)
    task.cancel()

asyncio.run(main())
```

How It Works

The first solution is the most obvious. A task is the instance of a future subclass and hence has a cancel method, which can be invoked to unschedule the corresponding coroutine from the event loop and abort it (if it's running).

This happens irrespective of what the current thread is. You can do this if you know that your application is single-threaded or you are absolutely sure that the loop you are handling is in fact on the same thread.

Solution #2

Another way to cancel a coroutine thread-safely is to use the loop.call_soon_threadsafe API in conjunction with the handle.cancel method.

```
import asyncio

async def cancellable(delay=10):
    loop = asyncio.get_running_loop()
    try:
        now = loop.time()
        print(f"Sleeping from {now} for {delay} seconds ...")
        await asyncio.sleep(delay)
        print(f"Slept for {delay} seconds without disturbance...")
    except asyncio.CancelledError:
        print(f"Cancelled at {now} after {loop.time()-now}
        seconds")

async def main():
    coro = cancellable()
    task = asyncio.create_task(coro)
    await asyncio.sleep(3)
```

```
    def canceller(task, fut):
        task.cancel()
        fut.set_result(None)

    loop = asyncio.get_running_loop()
    fut = loop.create_future()
    loop.call_soon_threadsafe(canceller, task, fut)
    await fut

asyncio.run(main())
```

How It Works

If you are on another thread, you can't safely schedule a callback with loop.call_soon or loop.call_at.

You need to use the loop.call_threadsafe method for that, which happens to be scheduled asynchronously as well.

To be able to tell when the scheduled coroutine has finished, you can pass a future object and call it at the right time and then await it on the outside.

Cancelling Multiple Coroutines

Problem

What if we want to cancel multiple scheduled coroutines at once? For instance, the coroutines iteratively build up some result. We either want to receive the result completely or stop the procedure, because the result has become irrelevant.

Here, we learn how to leverage asyncio.gather and asyncio. CancelledError to build an elegant solution that can do exactly that.

Solution

The `asyncio.gather` method is a high-level tool that can be used to group coroutines while silencing the emitted exceptions and returning them as a result value. The exceptions are returned by using the keyword-only argument `return_exceptions`.

```python
import asyncio

async def cancellable(delay=10, *, loop):
    try:
        now = loop.time()
        print(f"Sleeping from {now} for {delay} seconds ...")
        await asyncio.sleep(delay)
        print(f"Slept for {delay} seconds without disturbance...")
    except asyncio.CancelledError:
        print(f"Cancelled at {now} after {loop.time()-now}
        seconds")

def canceller(task, fut):
    task.cancel()
    fut.set_result(None)

async def cancel_threadsafe(gathered_tasks, loop):
    fut = loop.create_future()
    loop.call_soon_threadsafe(canceller, gathered_tasks, fut)
    await fut

async def main():
    loop = asyncio.get_running_loop()
    coros = [cancellable(i, loop=loop) for i in range(10)]

    gathered_tasks = asyncio.gather(*coros)
```

```
# Add a delay here, so we can see that the first three
coroutines run uninterrupted

await asyncio.sleep(3)

await cancel_threadsafe(gathered_tasks, loop)

try:
    await gathered_tasks
except asyncio.CancelledError:
    print("Was cancelled")
```

```
asyncio.run(main())
```

How It Works

Using asyncio.gather, we can do the following:

- Schedule all the coroutines passed to it concurrently

- Receive a GatheringFuture, which can be used to
  cancel all coroutines at the same time

If awaited successfully, asyncio.gather returns a list of all the results. asyncio.gather supports a keyword-only argument called return_exceptions, which can alter the result set on the GatheringFuture.

If an exception occurs in one of the scheduled coroutines, it can either bubble up or be returned as an argument.

Note Irrespective of the return_exceptions argument being set to True or not, the cancellation of the GatheringFuture is always propagated since Python 3.7.

Shielding a Coroutine from Cancellation
Problem

Some coroutines are vital to the integrity of the system and hence we cannot allow them to be cancelled by accident. For example, some initialization hooks of the system need to take place before we can run anything else. Therefore, we cannot allow them to be cancelled inadvertently.

Solution

If you want to ensure that a coroutine cannot be cancelled from the outside, you can use asyncio.shield.

```python
import asyncio

async def cancellable(delay=10):
    now = asyncio.get_running_loop().time()
    try:
        print(f"Sleeping from {now} for {delay} seconds ...")
        await asyncio.sleep(delay)
        print(f"Slept for {delay} seconds without disturbance...")
    except asyncio.CancelledError:
        print("I was disturbed in my sleep!")

def canceller(task, fut):
    task.cancel()
    fut.set_result(None)

async def cancel_threadsafe(task, *, delay=3, loop):
    await asyncio.sleep(delay)
    fut = loop.create_future()
    loop.call_soon_threadsafe(canceller, task, fut)
```

```
    await fut

async def main():
    complete_time = 10
    cancel_after_secs = 3
    loop=asyncio.get_running_loop()
    coro = cancellable(delay=complete_time)
    shielded_task = asyncio.shield(coro)
    asyncio.create_task(cancel_threadsafe(shielded_task,
    delay=cancel_after_secs, loop=loop))

    try:
        await shielded_task
    except asyncio.CancelledError:
        await asyncio.sleep(complete_time - cancel_after_secs)

asyncio.run(main())
```

How It Works

After shielding your task, you can safely call `cancel` on the shielded task without fearing that the coroutine/task that's shielded will also be cancelled.

Note that you cannot safeguard a coroutine from being cancelled from within itself with `asyncio.shield`. Given how `asyncio.shield` is implemented (in the Python 3.7 version), it will add another task to the global task list.

Hence, if you have shutdown logic that works along the lines of `gather(*all_tasks()).cancel()`, you might cancel the inner task of the shield operation.

Chaining Coroutines

Problem

Using concurrency does not mean our code is free from assumptions about ordering and consequence. In fact, it is even more essential to have a way to express them in an easily understandable fashion.

Solution

For that purpose, we can deploy the await keyword, which can be used to block the execution of awaitables until they either return or are cancelled.

```python
import asyncio

async def print_delayed(delay, text):
    print(await asyncio.sleep(delay, text))

async def main():
    await print_delayed(1, "Printing this after 1 second")
    await print_delayed(1, "Printing this after 2 seconds")
    await print_delayed(1, "Printing this after 3 seconds")

asyncio.run(main())
```

How It Works

Just one coroutine can run at the same time on a loop, since a coroutine runs also under the GIL.

We use the await keyword to schedule an *awaitable* on the loop with the premise of returning from that call when the awaitable has finished executing or has been cancelled.

Awaitables can be one of the following:

- A native coroutine object returned from a native coroutine function.

- A generator-based coroutine object returned from a function decorated with @asyncio.coroutine().

- An object with an __await__ method returning an iterator (futures fall in this category).

You can check for an awaitable by means of inspect.isawaitable.

Waiting on Multiple Coroutines
Problem

We want to wait on multiple coroutines at the same time.

Solution

We have two options to wait on multiple coroutines:

- asyncio.gather

- asyncio.wait

Both have their use cases. The asyncio.gather function provides a way to group and wait/cancel multiple coroutines at a time, as seen in the prior example.

If your only use case is to schedule multiple coroutines at the same time, you can safely assume that asyncio.gather is sufficient to do the job.

```python
import asyncio

async def print_delayed(delay, text,result):
    print(await asyncio.sleep(delay, text))
    return result

async def main():
    workload = [
        print_delayed(1, "Printing this after 1 second",1),
        print_delayed(1, "Printing this after 1 second",2),
        print_delayed(1, "Printing this after 1 second",3),
    ]

    results = await asyncio.gather(*workload)
    print(results)

asyncio.run(main())
```

How It Works

asyncio.gather schedules and executes multiple coroutines or futures using asyncio.ensure_future. This API is kept inside of Python 3.7 for backward compatibility. It uses asyncio.get_event_loop for querying the current event loop in the case of coroutines or asyncio.Future.get_loop in the case of futures before passing both of them to asyncio.ensure_future for scheduling.

Note   The entrance order is not necessarily the order in which the coroutines/futures are scheduled.

All futures must share the same event loop. If all the tasks are completed successfully, the returned future's result is the list of results (in the order of the original sequence, not necessarily the result order).

Additionally, there is the `return_exception` keyword-only argument, which we discussed in the "How to Cancel Multiple Coroutines" section.

Waiting on Multiple Coroutines with Different Heuristics

Problem

Recall that we talked about two ways to await multiple coroutines:

- `asyncio.gather`
- `asyncio.wait`

The one we have not discussed yet is `asyncio.wait`, which can be used to wait on multiple coroutines with different heuristics.

Solution #1

We will wait for multiple coroutines using `asyncio.wait` and `asyncio. ALL_COMPLETED`.

```python
import asyncio

async def raiser():
    raise Exception("An exception was raised")

async def main():
    raiser_future = asyncio.ensure_future(raiser())
    hello_world_future = asyncio.create_task(asyncio.sleep(1.0,
    "I have returned!"))
    coros = {raiser_future, hello_world_future}
    finished, pending = await asyncio.wait(coros, return_
    when=asyncio.ALL_COMPLETED)
```

```
    assert raiser_future in finished
    assert raiser_future not in pending
    assert hello_world_future in finished
    assert hello_world_future not in pending

    print(raiser_future.exception())
    print(hello_world_future.result())

asyncio.run(main())
```

Solution #2

We will wait for multiple coroutines using asyncio.wait and asyncio.
FIRST_EXCEPTION.

```
import asyncio

async def raiser():
    raise Exception("An exception was raised")

async def main():
    raiser_future = asyncio.ensure_future(raiser())
    hello_world_future = asyncio.create_task(asyncio.sleep(1.0,
    "I have returned!"))
    coros = {raiser_future, hello_world_future}
    finished, pending = await asyncio.wait(coros, return_
    when=asyncio.FIRST_EXCEPTION)

    assert raiser_future in finished
    assert raiser_future not in pending
    assert hello_world_future not in finished
    assert hello_world_future in pending

    print(raiser_future.exception())
    err_was_thrown = None
```

```
try:
    print(hello_world_future.result())
except asyncio.InvalidStateError as err:
    err_was_thrown = err
assert err_was_thrown

asyncio.run(main())
```

Solution #3

We will wait for multiple coroutines using asyncio.wait and asyncio.
FIRST_COMPLETED.

```
import asyncio

async def raiser():
    raise Exception("An exception was raised")

async def main():
    raiser_future = asyncio.ensure_future(raiser())
    hello_world_future = asyncio.create_task(asyncio.sleep(1.0,
    "I have returned!"))
    coros = {raiser_future, hello_world_future}
    finished, pending = await asyncio.wait(coros, return_
    when=asyncio.FIRST_COMPLETED)

    assert raiser_future in finished
    assert raiser_future not in pending
    assert hello_world_future not in finished
    assert hello_world_future in pending

    print(raiser_future.exception())
    err_was_thrown = None

    try:
        print(hello_world_future.result())
```

```
    except asyncio.InvalidStateError as err:
        err_was_thrown = err
    assert err_was_thrown

asyncio.run(main())
```

How It Works

The different solutions of this section demonstrate how `asyncio.wait` behaves with different values of the `return_when` parameter.

`asyncio.wait` is more low level than `asyncio.gather` in the sense that it can be used for grouping coroutines as well, but not for cancellation purposes. It takes a keyword-only parameter called `return_when` with the wait strategy. It returns with two values—two sets either containing the finished and the pending tasks.

The allowed values for the `return_when` parameter are as follows:

- `FIRST_COMPLETED`: Returns when any future finishes or is cancelled.

- `FIRST_EXCEPTION`: Returns when any future finishes by raising an exception. If no future raises an exception, then this value is equivalent to `ALL_COMPLETED`.

- `ALL_COMPLETED`: Returns when all futures finish or are cancelled.

Note   You should not pass coroutines directly to `asyncio.wait` but rather wrap them in a task first via `asyncio.create_task` or `loop.create_task`. The reason for this is that coroutines are wrapped inside of `asyncio.wait` using `ensure_future`. `ensure_future` leaves future instances unchanged. It is not possible to use the coroutines to check inside the returned sets of `asyncio.wait` - which are (done, pending), for the status of the coroutines.

We added the asserts to illustrate how asyncio.wait behaves given the possible values for the return_when parameter.

Note   Just calling raiser_future.exception() is not a safe option, since it might raise a CancelledError.

Waiting on Multiple Coroutines and Ignoring Exceptions

Problem

We know so far that we have two ways of running multiple coroutines and waiting on them, which are:

- asyncio.gather

- asyncio.wait

In both cases, we need to ensure that the future that gathers all the coroutines/tasks is not cancelled.

We also how to achieve cancellation safety, which is to use asyncio.shield.

Solution

Now we learn now how all that knowledge comes together to wait on multiple coroutines and ignore exceptions using asyncio.gather and asyncio.shield:

```
import asyncio
import sys

async def print_delayed(delay, text, ):
    print(await asyncio.sleep(delay, text))
```

```
async def raise_delayed(delay, text, ):
    raise Exception(await asyncio.sleep(delay, text))

async def main():
    workload = [
        print_delayed(5, "Printing this after 5 seconds"),
        raise_delayed(5, "Raising this after 5 seconds"),
        print_delayed(5, "Printing this after 5 seconds"),
    ]

    res = None
    try:
        gathered = asyncio.gather(*workload, return_
        exceptions=True)
        res = await gathered
    except asyncio.CancelledError:
        print("The gathered task was cancelled", file=sys.stderr)
    finally:
        print("Result:", res)

asyncio.run(main())
```

How It Works

We schedule our workload using the asyncio.gather function; note that
we also schedule a coroutine that will raise an exception.

To shield against premature cancellation of our GatheringFuture, we
wrap everything into a try except block since asyncio.shield has no effect.

Note   The try except block just stops the CancelledError from
bubbling up and the coroutines behind the GatheringFuture get
cancelled nonetheless.

Setting `return_exceptions` to `True`, however, turns all exceptions (also `CancelledErrors`) into return values. You can find them in the corresponding position of the returned list.

Waiting for a Specific Condition

Problem

We want to create a simple API that allows us to wait for a coroutine if a condition of choice is invalid. Ideally, the API will allow us to pass our condition as a predicate function.

Solution

asyncio provides an implementation of condition variables, a synchronization primitive. They enable coroutines to wait until a condition occurs.

```python
import asyncio

async def execute_on(condition, coro, predicate):
    async with condition:
        await condition.wait_for(predicate)
        await coro

async def print_coro(text):
    print(text)

async def worker(numbers):
    while numbers:
        print("Numbers:", numbers)
        numbers.pop()
        await asyncio.sleep(0.25)
```

```
async def main():
    numbers = list(range(10))
    condition = asyncio.Condition()
    is_empty = lambda: not numbers
    await worker(numbers)
    await execute_on(condition, print_coro("Finished!"), is_empty)

asyncio.run(main())
```

How It Works

We can use a `condition` variable to monitor the completion of our worker
coroutine, which pops the numbers inside the numbers list one after
another.

Condition variables provide us with implicit and explicit notifying.
Either they monitor a predicate that's called repeatedly until it becomes
true or the waiters are notified by calling `condition_variable.notify` or
`condition_variable.notify_all.`

The example uses `implicit notifying.` Hence, our predicate
function, which is `is_empty = lambda: not numbers`, must return `True`
for the condition variable's lock to be freed.

We define the helper coroutine function `execute_on`, which sets the
lock inside the condition variable correctly. This happens before we use
the `wait_for` coroutine method to wait until the predicate holds true and
dispatch the passed coroutine.

Note   If you use the condition variable in more than one coroutine,
you need to pass your own `asyncio.Lock` instance!

CHAPTER 4

Working with Async Generators

Let's recap which problems conventional generators try to solve.

We have a complex computation that can be performed iteratively and are interested in every sub-result along the way. Of course, we could pre-compute all values up to the desired value. But that means we would have to wait until we reached the desired value to return a collection of values pre-populated with the previous sub-results. This is because returning from a function means we would lose all of the "context" that it held up to that point.

Fortunately, Python provides the native and clean API of generators to be able to return sub-results/values without losing the generator function's "context." An issue remains with the *generator* pattern. If the computations for the sub-results are independent, we unnecessarily provide the results in the order of the yield calls.

This is a result of our generators working in a synchronous fashion. If we asynchronously compute the steps and always return the result that has finished computing as the next value, we basically have the framework for our async generator.

© Mohamed Mustapha Tahrioui 2019
M. M. Tahrioui, *asyncio Recipes*, https://doi.org/10.1007/978-1-4842-4401-2_4

Writing an Async Generator

Problem

You can use async generators when you need to asynchronously generate a sequence of values and have the construct behave like an iterator.

Solution

Async generators are the logical extension to (synchronous) generators. The asynchronous generator iterators are governed under the asynchronous iterator protocol. The asynchronous iterator protocol can be implemented by providing the __aiter__ method and the __anext__ coroutine method or by writing an asynchronous generator function.

The __aiter__ method returns the asynchronous iterator and is synchronous.

The __anext__ coroutine method returns an *awaitable* object, which uses a StopIteration exception to "yield" values and an StopAsyncIteration exception to signal the end of the iteration. Asynchronous generator functions look like native coroutine /async-def functions and return an asynchronous generator iterator. They hence may contain "yield" expressions for producing values that can be consumed by an async-for loop.

To demonstrate how an asynchronous generator function is written, we will write an asynchronous generator that generates random numbers that yield control to the event loop for a specified time.

```
import random
import asyncio

async def random_number_gen(delay,start,end):
    while True:
        yield random.randint(start,end)
        await asyncio.sleep(delay)
```

How It Works

The async random number generator is written as you would expect from a synchronous one.

You pass it an interval via the start and end parameters, and it will generate random integers using the random module.

The catch is that the coroutine yields control to the event loop for delay seconds after generating the number to not block other coroutines.

The implications are that the consumers of random_number_gen need to be order-agnostic—meaning they need to be independent of each other in terms of which consumer finishes first/last.

If you prefer an order preserving but blocking scheme, delete await asyncio.sleep(delay) and the delay parameter - which would be equivalent to a synchronous generator.

Running an Async Generator

Problem

Async generators cannot be awaited like normal coroutines. This section shows how they can be run.

Solution

Consuming an async generator is possible two ways:

- Using an async for loop

- Manually interacting with the async generator by means of the asend and aclose coroutines on it

The first option is more high level and what you want to run in a production setting. There might be reasons why you decide otherwise. For instance, using the async generator as a pausable/resumable coroutine that you can feed data to after scheduling and that preserves context/state. We will use this feature in the state machine section.

```
import random
import asyncio

async def random_number_gen(delay,start,end):
    while True:
        yield random.randint(start,end)
        await asyncio.sleep(delay)

async def main():

    async for i in random_number_gen(1,0,100):
        print(i)
try:
    print("Starting to print out random numbers...")
    print("Shut down the application with Ctrl+C")
    asyncio.run(main())
except KeyboardInterrupt:
    print("Closed the main loop..")
```

How It Works

To demonstrate how to run an async generator, we run our example random_number_gen in the main coroutine. We schedule the main coroutine via asyncio.run and make sure we can catch a KeyboardInterrupt to have a way to exit the loop. asyncio.run cleans up async generators that haven't finished executing (such as the while-True-loop based random_number_gen async generator).

Wrapping an Async Generator in an Async Comprehension

Problem

Async generators enhance generators that can be consumed in comprehension statements. Likewise, you can consume async generators in async comprehension statements.

Solution

To demonstrate how to wrap an async generator in an async comprehension, we will write a non-blocking multi-server HTTP client that can request the contents of multiple URLs seamlessly, using only standard library components.

We deploy the asynchronous comprehension in the part that generates the non-blocking request objects using the loop.run_in_executor API. We use urllib3 as a blocking HTTP client library, which we will asyncify. Hence, you need to install the certifi and urllib3 packages via the package manager of your choice. For example, via pip or pipenv, you use:

```
pip3 install urllib3==1.23
pip3 install certifi==2018.04.16
# or
pipenv install urllib3==1.23
pipenv install certifi==2018.04.16
```

Note   In this example, we use the certifi module for collections of root certificates that we can use to query TLS-secured websites over HTTPS.

```python
import asyncio
import functools
from concurrent.futures.thread import ThreadPoolExecutor

import sys
import certifi
import urllib3

async def request(poolmanager: urllib3.PoolManager,
                  executor,
                  *,
                  method="GET",
                  url,
                  fields=None,
                  headers=None,
                  loop: asyncio.AbstractEventLoop = None, ):
    if not loop:
        loop = asyncio.get_running_loop()
    request = functools.partial(poolmanager.request, method,
    url, fields=fields, headers=headers)
    return  loop.run_in_executor(executor, request)

async def bulk_requests(poolmanager: urllib3.PoolManager,
                  executor,
                  *,
                  method="GET",
                  urls,
                  fields=None,
                  headers=None,
                  loop: asyncio.AbstractEventLoop = None, ):
    for url in urls:
        yield await request(poolmanager, executor, url=url,
        fields=fields, headers=headers, loop=loop)
```

```python
def filter_unsuccesful_requests(responses_and_exceptions):
    return filter(
        lambda url_and_response: not isinstance(url_and_
        response[1], Exception),
        responses_and_exceptions.items()
    )

async def main():
    poolmanager = urllib3.PoolManager(cert_reqs='CERT_
    REQUIRED', ca_certs=certifi.where())
    executor = ThreadPoolExecutor(10)
    urls = [
        "https://google.de",
        "https://apple.com",
        "https://apress.com",
    ]
    requests = [request async for request in bulk_
    requests(poolmanager, executor, urls=urls, )]
    responses_and_exceptions = dict(zip(urls, await asyncio.
    gather(*requests, return_exceptions=True)))
    responses = {url: resp.data for (url, resp) in filter_
    unsuccesful_requests(responses_and_exceptions)}

    for res in responses.items():
        print(res)

    for url in urls:
        if url not in responses:
            print(f"No successful request could be
            made to {url}. Reason: {responses_and_
            exceptions[url]}",file=sys.stderr)

asyncio.run(main())
```

How It Works

We start by writing a non-blocking wrapper around the urllib3. PoolManager API. For this purpose, we schedule the poolmanager.request method on an executor via the loop.run_in_executor coroutine method. The convenience function request encapsulates that logic and has the same signature (and defaults) as poolmanager.request.

Note that this is prone to error in between Python versions since the underlying API might change!

---

bulk_requests is our async generator. It iterates over a list of URLs and returns the futures that will resolve to the content under the URLs if the request was successful. To collect all the request futures, we deploy an async list comprehension. The syntax follows a synchronous comprehension with an additional async keyword in front of the loop.

Similar comprehensions exist for dicts and sets. We then go on to dispatch the requests via asyncio.gather and filter out the unsuccessful events. An error message is printed for every failed request.

Writing a State Machine with an Async Generator

Problem

You can use the async generator interface to interact with an async generator, thereby turning it into a state machine.

Solution

Given the nature of async generators—which is that they preserve the coroutine's state and that they can be communicated with by means of asend—we can manually iterate over them by means of asend calls for every step.

We will write a state machine that is controlled by a user prompt which invokes the respective events.

```python
import asyncio
import enum
import logging
import sys
from dataclasses import dataclass

class State(enum.Enum):
    IDLE = enum.auto()
    STARTED = enum.auto()
    PAUSED = enum.auto()

@dataclass(frozen=True)
class Event:
    name: str

START = Event("Start")
PAUSE = Event("Pause")
STOP = Event("Stop")
EXIT = Event("Exit")

STATES = (START, PAUSE, STOP, EXIT)
CHOICES = "\n".join([f"{i}: {state.name}" for i, state in
enumerate(STATES)])

MENU = f"""
Menu

Enter your choice:

{CHOICES}

"""
```

```python
TRANSITIONS = {
    (State.IDLE, PAUSE): State.IDLE,
    (State.IDLE, START): State.STARTED,
    (State.IDLE, STOP): State.IDLE,

    (State.STARTED, START): State.STARTED,
    (State.STARTED, PAUSE): State.PAUSED,
    (State.STARTED, STOP): State.IDLE,

    (State.PAUSED, START): State.STARTED,
    (State.PAUSED, PAUSE): State.PAUSED,
    (State.PAUSED, STOP): State.IDLE,

    (State.IDLE, EXIT): State.IDLE,
    (State.STARTED, EXIT): State.IDLE,
    (State.PAUSED, EXIT): State.IDLE,
}

class StateMachineException(Exception):
    pass

class StartStateMachineException(StateMachineException):
    pass

class StopStateMachineException(StateMachineException):
    pass

async def next_state(state_machine, event, *,
exc=StateMachineException):
    try:
        if state_machine:
            await state_machine.asend(event)
    except StopAsyncIteration:
        if exc != StopStateMachineException:
            raise exc()
```

```
    except:
        raise exc()

async def start_statemachine(state_machine, ):
    await next_state(state_machine, None, exc=StartStateMachine
    Exception)

async def stop_statemachine(state_machine, ):
    await next_state(state_machine, EXIT,
    exc=StopStateMachineException)

async def create_state_machine(transitions, *, logger=None, ):
    if not logger:
        logger = logging.getLogger(__name__)
    event, current_state = None, State.IDLE
    while event != EXIT:

        event = yield

        edge = (current_state, event)

        if edge not in transitions:
            logger.error("Cannot consume %s in state %s",
            event.name, current_state.name)
            continue

        next_state = transitions.get(edge)
        logger.debug("Transitioning from %s to %s", current_
        state.name, next_state.name)
        current_state = next_state

def pick_next_event(logger):
    next_state = None
```

```python
    while not next_state:
        try:
            next_state = STATES[int(input(MENU))]
        except (ValueError, IndexError):
            logger.error("Please enter a valid choice!")
            continue

    return next_state

async def main(logger):
    state_machine = create_state_machine(TRANSITIONS,
    logger=logger)

    try:
        await start_statemachine(state_machine)

        while True:
            event = pick_next_event(logger)
            if event != EXIT:
                await next_state(state_machine, event)
            else:
                await stop_statemachine(state_machine)

    except StartStateMachineException:
        logger.error("Starting the statemachine was
        unsuccessful")
    except StopStateMachineException:
        logger.error("Stopping the statemachine was
        unsuccessful")
    except StateMachineException:
        logger.error("Transitioning the statemachine was
        unsuccessful")
```

```
logger = logging.getLogger(__name__)
logger.addHandler(logging.StreamHandler(sys.stdout))
logger.setLevel(logging.DEBUG)

try:
    asyncio.get_event_loop().run_until_complete(main(logger))
except KeyboardInterrupt:
    logger.info("Closed loop..")
```

How It Works

At the heart of a state machine lies a function that defines how to perform a transition from the current state given the input to another state. In our case, it's next_state.

next_state encapsulates the state transition logic and catches the StopAsyncIteration, which is thrown when we call aclose on the generator. A table that defines the valid transitions that might occur is also needed—and provided—via the TRANSITIONS dict.

We model the state events as data classes and the state as an enum. The user is prompted via the pick_next_event function, which presents a menu matching the possible events to invoke on the state machine. The current state will be printed. If an invalid transition was invoked, we raise a custom StateMachineException to inform the user something went wrong.

Additionally, we define convenience methods for starting, stopping, and creating the state machine. create_state_machine returns an async generator and waits for I/O until needed. It ignores the events in relation to unknown transitions.

Cleaning Up After Using Async Generators

Problem

Async generators may be stuck in execution when the loop changes state to stopped or cancelled.

Solution

To be able to properly stop the async generator, the `aclose` property of the async generator throws a `GeneratorExit` exception into the underlying generator.

The loop and the asyncio module provide two ways to cleanly address the issue when confronted with multiple async generators.

Option 1

```python
import asyncio

async def async_gen_coro():
    yield 1
    yield 2
    yield 3

async def main():
    async_generator = async_gen_coro()
    await async_generator.asend(None)
    await async_generator.asend(None)

asyncio.run(main())
```

How It Works

asyncio.BaseEventLoop provides the BaseEventLoop.shutdown_
asyncgens API, which schedules aclose calls on all the running async
generators.

asyncio.run conveniently handles calling loop.shutdown_asyncgens
for us internally.

Option 2

```
import asyncio

async def endless_async_gen():
    while True:
        yield 3
        await asyncio.sleep(1)

async def main():
    async for i in endless_async_gen():
        print(i)

loop = asyncio.new_event_loop()
asyncio.set_event_loop(loop)

try:
    loop.run_until_complete(main())
except KeyboardInterrupt:
    print("Caught Ctrl+C. Exiting now..")
finally:
    try:
        loop.run_until_complete(loop.shutdown_asyncgens())
    finally:
        loop.close()
```

How It Works

If you feel that you want to call BaseEvent.shutdown_asyncgens yourself at a point where your code will not spawn any new async generators, you can deploy a more elaborate shutdown routine. The principle stays the same: You need to put your loop.shutdown_asyncgens into the finally block of the try-except-finally construct around your loop.run_until_complete/loop.run_forever, since you want it to irrespective of any exception that your loop might have encountered.

Wring an Asynchronous Generator Based Web Crawler

Problem

We want to build a web based crawler that can exploit the CPU time most efficiently using async generators.

Solution

A web crawler is a piece of software that systematically browses the web. This means it starts at a point like an URL and traverses all the links that it encounters. If a web crawler operates in a synchronous fashion, it might block other tasks that may be executed while it waits for the responses to its requests. An async generator can yield control to the event loop at this point to better exploit the CPU time.

```
import asyncio

import re

import typing
```

```
from concurrent.futures import Executor, ThreadPoolExecutor

from urllib.request import urlopen

DEFAULT_EXECUTOR = ThreadPoolExecutor(4)
ANCHOR_TAG_PATTERN = re.compile(b"<a.+?href=[\"|\'](.*?)
[\"|\'].*?>", re.RegexFlag.MULTILINE | re.RegexFlag.IGNORECASE)

async def wrap_async(generator: typing.Generator,
                     executor: Executor = DEFAULT_EXECUTOR,
                     sentinel=object(),
                     *,
                     loop: asyncio.AbstractEventLoop = None):
    """
    We wrap a generator and return an asynchronous generator
    instead
    :param iterator:
    :param executor:
    :param sentinel:
    :param loop:
    :return:
    """

    if not loop:
        loop = asyncio.get_running_loop()

    while True:
        result = await loop.run_in_executor(executor, next,
        generator, sentinel)
        if result == sentinel:
            break
        yield result
```

```python
def follow(*links):
    """

    :param links:
    :return:
    """

    return ((link, urlopen(link).read()) for link in links)
def get_links(text: str):
    """

    Get back an iterator that gets us all the links in a text
    iteratively and safely
    :param text:
    :return:
    """

    # Always grab the last match, because that is how a smart
    # http parser would interpret a malformed # anchor tag
    return (match.groups()[-1]
            for match in ANCHOR_TAG_PATTERN.finditer(text)
            # This portion is a safeguard against None matches
            and zero href matches
            if hasattr(match, "groups") and len(match.groups())))
async def main(*links):
    async for current, body in wrap_async(follow(*links)):
        print("Current url:", current)
        print("Content:", body)
        async for link in wrap_async(get_links(body)):
            print(link)

asyncio.run(main("http://apress.com"))
```

How It Works

Our crawler focuses on the two main tasks—requesting a website and extracting all the links that it needs to follow. Both tasks involve a lot of I/O. We can offload this to a thread pool, where things can happen in parallel (so the tasks don't block each other) by using the `loop.run_in_executor` API. For that matter, `wrap_async` was written.

Note   Alternatively we can use a network module that is asyncio enabled like aiohttp which is not in the scope of this example.

Inside it, we invoke the `next` builtin, which takes a generator and a default value which will be returned if a StopIteration exception is thrown. We pass a sentinel object which we can test against later. This construction will iterate over the generator until it is exhausted and return the sentinel at which point the async generator will be closed by the `if result == sentinel:` condition. Since the `loop.run_in_executor` method returns a future, we need to await it to get the result. This function ensures that every step of the generator is executed non-blocking.

We need to create two generators now that follow links and another one that extracts links from a website:

- `follow` reads the contents of an URL uses `urllib` for multiple links

- `get_links` extracts the links of a multiple HTML page using a regex iterator

Each of these steps will be scheduled on the thread pool, thanks to `loop.run_in_executor` on `next`. The async generator will be then consumed in `main`, where we in turn print the found links and the current URL/body.

CHAPTER 5

Working with Async Context Manager

Context managers provide a convenient API to govern a runtime context. They expose the ability to hook into entering the context manager scope and exit it. Given that asyncio extends the language with the possibility of execution suspension, it becomes evident that a synchronous context manager cannot interface with the event loop in a seamless fashion.

An asynchronous context manager is a context manager that can use the await keyword to suspend execution in its enter and exit methods. This way, it can yield control back to the event loop and interact with resources (like a database) in an asynchronous fashion.

The asynchronous context manager was introduced in the course of PEP-0492 and uses a pattern we already now from the async generator. Well-known APIs like the for loop are used in conjunction with the async keyword. In the case of the async context manager the with keyword will be prefixed with the async keyword.

To not convolute the context manager API, it was decided that all the bits used in the context manager protocol would be replicated for the asynchronous context rather than reused.

For instance, the dunder methods __enter__ and __exit__ are copied as __aenter__ and __aexit__ for the asynchronous variant.

Note that __aenter__ and __aexit__ need to be coroutine methods. For Python version 3.7 and with the help of native coroutines, it is now possible to use an asynchronous generator and the asynccontextmanager decorator jointly to adhere to the asynchronous context manager protocol.

Writing an Async Context Manager

As of Python 3.7, there are two ways to write an async context manager. Similar to the synchronous context manager, we can either write a class and override the __aenter__ and __aexit__ coroutine methods or use the asynccontextmanager decorator.

Solution

In this solution we'll put the asynccontextmanager decorator to use by writing an asynchronous context manager that enables non-blocking file I/O.

```python
from concurrent.futures.thread import ThreadPoolExecutor
from contextlib import asynccontextmanager
import asyncio

class AsyncFile(object):

    def __init__(self, file, loop=None, executor=None):
        if not loop:
            loop = asyncio.get_running_loop()
        if not executor:
            executor = ThreadPoolExecutor(10)
        self.file = file
        self.loop = loop
        self.executor = executor
        self.pending = []
        self.result = []
```

```python
    def write(self, string):
        self.pending.append(
            self.loop.run_in_executor(self.executor, self.file.
            write, string, )
        )

    def read(self, i):
        self.pending.append(
            self.loop.run_in_executor(self.executor, self.file.
            read, i, )
        )

    def readlines(self):
        self.pending.append(
            self.loop.run_in_executor(self.executor, self.file.
            readlines, )
        )

@asynccontextmanager
async def async_open(path, mode="w"):
    with open(path, mode=mode) as f:
        loop = asyncio.get_running_loop()
        file = AsyncFile(f, loop=loop)
        try:
            yield file
        finally:
            file.result = await asyncio.gather(*file.pending,
            loop=loop)
```

How It Works

Leveraging our knowledge about asynchronous generators and the context manager returned by the call to open, we can write an asynchronous generator function that returns a non-blocking wrapper around our file handle.

The AsyncFile class provides methods that add the calls to write, read, and readlines to a list of pending tasks. These tasks are scheduled on a ThreadPoolExecutor through an event loop in the finally block.

The finally block corresponds to __aexit__ in this case since it is ensured to be run; it also happens after the yield of the AsyncFile object.

This way, we achieve non-blocking file I/O in the context of the asynchronous context manager.

Note that the results of the read calls will be stored in the result field of the AsyncFile object.

Running an Async Context Manager

Given our asynchronous context manager from the previous example, we want to leverage the async with keywords to schedule the async context manager.

Solution

Using the async with keywords, we can enter the runtime context of an async context manager.

Note   The async with syntax can only be used inside a coroutine function.

Upon entering the async context manager scope, the __aenter__ coroutine method is called without parameters and upon leaving, the __aexit__ coroutine method is called with the following parameters: exception type, exception value, and traceback object.

Note   The parameters passed to __aexit__ are optional and may be set to None if no exception occurred.

```python
import asyncio
import tempfile
import os

async def main():
    tempdir = tempfile.gettempdir()
    path = os.path.join(tempdir, "run.txt")
    print(f"Writing asynchronously to {path}")

    async with async_open(path, mode="w") as f:
        f.write("This\n")
        f.write("might\n")
        f.write("not\n")
        f.write("end\n")
        f.write("up\n")
        f.write("in\n")
        f.write("the\n")
        f.write("same\n")
        f.write("order!\n")

asyncio.run(main())
```

How It Works

Since the async context manager uses the `async` keyword, it can only be used in the context of a (native) coroutine method.

The syntax is simply `async with` followed by the call to the asynchronous context manager and, eventually, an `as` directive. The rest is similar to synchronous context managers.

Synchronizing Pending Coroutines to Finish Cleanly

asyncio provides multiple APIs to use if you want to await pending coroutines.

There are APIs that target single and multiple coroutines and some that enable the developer to await the coroutines under certain conditions or iteratively.

We want to learn how to use these APIs in conjunction with async context managers to synchronize pending coroutines cleanly.

Solution

For awaiting coroutines, the following APIs can be used in conjunction with the `await` keyword: `asyncio.gather`, `asyncio.wait`, `asyncio.wait_for`, and `as_completed`.

But this step needs to happen manually. Using async context managers, we can write thin wrappers around these functions to create powerful high-level synchronization tools.

The next solution demonstrates a synchronization wall, after which we can expect all scheduled coroutines to have finished.

```python
import asyncio

class Sync():
    def __init__(self):
        self.pending = []
        self.finished = None

    def schedule_coro(self, coro, shield=False):
        fut = asyncio.shield(coro) if shield else asyncio.
        ensure_future(coro)
        self.pending.append(fut)
        return fut

    async def __aenter__(self):
        return self

    async def __aexit__(self, exc_type, exc_val, exc_tb):
        self.finished = await asyncio.gather(*self.pending,
        return_exceptions=True)

async def workload():
    await asyncio.sleep(3)
    print("These coroutines will be executed simultaneously and
    return 42")
    return 42

async def main():
    async with Sync() as sync:
        sync.schedule_coro(workload())
        sync.schedule_coro(workload())
        sync.schedule_coro(workload())
    print("All scheduled coroutines have retuned or thrown:",
    sync.finished)

asyncio.run(main())
```

How It Works

Given our knowledge of `asyncio.gather` and the async context manager protocol, we can build a component that schedules work and awaits upon leaving the scope.

For this matter, we wrote the async context manager called Sync, which exposes a `schedule_coro` method that can be used to schedule work (in the form of a coroutine) and eventually shield it. It is then added to a list.

After all the work has been scheduled and protected from cancellation, we can await it cleanly via `asyncio.gather`. Note that `asyncio.shield` schedules the workload. So the work is already running and is a task object at that point.

Given that passing non-tasks to `asyncio.gather` is deprecated, this is the intended behavior.

Note that you need to use the task object returned by `schedule_coro` for identity comparisons!

Interacting Asynchronously with a Closeable Resource

You might have to deal with resources that schedule their close action as a concurrent action.

Solution

Under the premise that asynchronously closing resources while exposing a future allows us to stall the actual closing of the resource, we can write an async context manager that abstracts the cleanup/closing away.

```
import asyncio
import socket
from contextlib import asynccontextmanager
```

```python
@asynccontextmanager
async def tcp_client(host='google.de', port=80):
    address_info = (await asyncio.get_running_loop().getaddrinfo(
        host, port,
        proto=socket.IPPROTO_TCP,
    )).pop()

    if not address_info:
        raise ValueError(f"Could not resolve {host}:{port}")
    host,port =address_info[-1]
    reader, writer = await asyncio.open_connection(host, port)
    try:
        yield (reader, writer)
    finally:
        writer.close()
        await asyncio.shield(writer.wait_closed())

async def main():
    async with tcp_client() as (reader, writer):
        writer.write(b"GET /us HTTP/1.1\r\nhost: apress.com\r\n\r\n")
        await writer.drain()
        content = await reader.read(1024**2)
        print(content)

asyncio.run(main())
```

How It Works

asyncio provides us with a high-level tool called `asyncio.open_connection` to open an asynchronous stream writer and reader on an URL with a given port.

The writer needs to be closed properly to deallocate the sockets opened in the course of the connection.

Otherwise, both connection parties remain in a state of connection (disregarding premature disconnections due to errors).

We can close a writer with the `close` method, but until the `wait_closed` awaitable is awaited, we cannot safely assume it is closed.

We shield awaiting `writer.wait_closed` so that it cannot be cancelled from the outside.

Given that we close and await the writer in the `finally` block, we can safely assume that both actions succeed or that exceptions raised inside the writer bubble up.

Writing a Loop Worker Pool Async Context Manager

Given our knowledge of how to build an async context manager that synchronizes all the coroutines scheduled inside its scope after leaving *and* how to build custom event loops, we know how to write a loop worker pool async context manager that ensures that all the `loop.call_*` callbacks have finished after leaving its scope.

Solution

In Chapter 2, "Event Loop," we discussed a way to await synchronous actions on the loop by writing our own loop implementation.

You might remember learning about the `await_callbacks` method, which needs to be awaited to make sure all the scheduled handles have finished.

We will leverage the same loop implementation in conjunction with the async context manager protocol to build a coroutine worker pool async context manager.

```python
import asyncio
from contextlib import asynccontextmanager
from functools import partial as func

class SchedulerLoop(asyncio.SelectorEventLoop):

    def __init__(self):
        super(SchedulerLoop, self).__init__()
        self._scheduled_callback_futures = []
        self.results = []

    @staticmethod
    def unwrapper(fut: asyncio.Future, function):
        """

        Function to get rid of the implicit fut parameter.
        :param fut:
        :type fut:
        :param function:
        :return:
        """

        return function()

    def _future(self, done_hook):
        """

        Create a future object that calls the done_hook when it
        is awaited
        :param loop:
        :param function:
        :return:
        """

        fut = self.create_future()
        fut.add_done_callback(func(self.unwrapper,
        function=done_hook))
        return fut
```

```python
    def schedule_soon_threadsafe(self, callback, *args,
    context=None):
        fut = self._future(func(callback, *args))
        self._scheduled_callback_futures.append(fut)
        self.call_soon_threadsafe(fut.set_result, None,
        context=context)

    def schedule_soon(self, callback, *args, context=None):
        fut = self._future(func(callback, *args))
        self._scheduled_callback_futures.append(fut)
        self.call_soon(fut.set_result, None, context=context)

    def schedule_later(self, delay_in_seconds, callback, *args,
    context=None):
        fut = self._future(func(callback, *args))
        self._scheduled_callback_futures.append(fut)
        self.call_later(delay_in_seconds, fut.set_result, None,
        context=context)

    def schedule_at(self, delay_in_seconds, callback, *args,
    context=None):
        fut = self._future(func(callback, *args))
        self._scheduled_callback_futures.append(fut)
        self.call_at(delay_in_seconds, fut.set_result, None,
        context=context)

    async def await_callbacks(self):
        callback_futs = self._scheduled_callback_futures[:]
        self._scheduled_callback_futures[:] = []
        return await asyncio.gather(*callback_futs, return_
        exceptions=True, loop=self)
```

```
class SchedulerLoopPolicy(asyncio.DefaultEventLoopPolicy):
    def new_event_loop(self):
        return SchedulerLoop()

@asynccontextmanager
async def scheduler_loop():
    loop = asyncio.get_running_loop()
    if not isinstance(loop, SchedulerLoop):
        raise ValueError("You can run the scheduler_loop async
        context manager only on a SchedulerLoop")

    try:
        yield loop
    finally:
        loop.results = await loop.await_callbacks()

async def main():
    async with scheduler_loop() as loop:
        loop.schedule_soon(print, "This")
        loop.schedule_soon(print, "works")
        loop.schedule_soon(print, "seamlessly")

asyncio.set_event_loop_policy(SchedulerLoopPolicy())
asyncio.run(main())
```

How It Works

scheduler_loop is our async context manager and it makes sure that the
loop we are running is a SchedulerLoop.

It fetches the currently running loop and awaits loop.await_
callbacks in its __aexit__ part/finally block.

To use the convenience of the asyncio.run API, we write a small
LoopPolicy where we override the loop.new_event_loop method to
return a SchedulerLoop instance.

Next, we run the main coroutine to see our async context manager scheduler_loop in action.

Writing a Subprocess Worker Pool Async Context Manager

Leveraging many patterns we have already learned, we can write an async context manager that schedules functions on different processes and runs on our event loop.

Solution

Using the asyncio.wrap_future method, which is intended to wrap concurrent.futures.Future objects into awaitable asyncio.Future objects, we can interact with the multiprocessing package. It is discouraged to pass a ProcessPoolExecutor to the loop.run_in_executor API (since a loop that is configured to use it may throw an OSError on loop.close—see https://bugs.python.org/issue34073 for more information). Instead, the preferred method is to use the asyncio.wrap_future and executor.submit APIs together.

```python
import asyncio
from concurrent.futures.process import ProcessPoolExecutor
from contextlib import asynccontextmanager
from multiprocessing import get_context, freeze_support

CONTEXT = get_context("spawn")

class AsyncProcessPool:

    def __init__(self, executor, loop=None, ):
        self.executor = executor
```

```
        if not loop:
            loop = asyncio.get_running_loop()
        self.loop = loop
        self.pending = []
        self.result = None

    def submit(self, fn, *args, **kwargs):
        fut = asyncio.wrap_future(self.executor.submit(fn,
        *args, **kwargs), loop=self.loop)
        self.pending.append(fut)
        return fut

@asynccontextmanager
async def pool(max_workers=None, mp_context=CONTEXT,
               initializer=None, initargs=(), loop=None, return_
               exceptions=True):
    with ProcessPoolExecutor(max_workers=max_workers, mp_
    context=mp_context,
                                initializer=initializer,
                                initargs=initargs) as executor:
        pool = AsyncProcessPool(executor, loop=loop)
        try:
            yield pool
        finally:
            pool.result = await asyncio.gather(*pool.pending,
            loop=pool.loop, return_exceptions=return_exceptions)

async def main():
    async with pool() as p:
        p.submit(print, "This works perfectly fine")
        result = await p.submit(sum, (1, 2))
        print(result)
    print(p.result)
```

```
if __name__ == '__main__':
    freeze_support()
    asyncio.run(main())
```

How It Works

Given that a ProcessPoolExecutor has a submit method that returns
concurrent.futures.Future objects, we can write an AsyncProcessPool
that provides us with an analogue submit method that works on an event
loop by using asyncio.wrap_future on the return value.

By saving the scheduled tasks, we can await them in the finally block
of our async context manager.

Using asyncio.wrap_future, we can safely interact with the results of
a subprocess computation result in an asyncio way. We can use ayncio.
wait_for for timeouts or shield them from cancellation with asyncio.
shield (given that nothing cancels the subprocess from within).

When we fall out of the pool scope, all the scheduled workloads will
have finished.

Additionally, if we need to make stronger assurances inside the async
context manager scope, we can manually await them.

CHAPTER 6

Communication Between Asyncio Components

In the previous chapters, we learned about asynchronous interfaces to standard library components (or even completely new APIs) that, in the broader sense, keep shareable state/context or are "runnable". This includes:

- Coroutines

- Tasks

- Async generators

- Async context managers

- Async comprehensions

- Subprocesses

These components might need to share their state with other instances of asyncio components. Examples where this makes sense include:

- Coroutine workers

- State-machine or state-keeping coroutines, such as an audio player (playing/paused/idle)

© Mohamed Mustapha Tahrioui 2019
M. M. Tahrioui, *asyncio Recipes*, https://doi.org/10.1007/978-1-4842-4401-2_6

- A watchdog for multiple subprocesses

- Synchronization of distributed computations

To facilitate shared state/context, asyncio provides counterparts of processes/thread communication, tools like queues and signals. Asyncio also influenced the creation of new APIs, like *contextvars,* which are intended to provide the semantic equivalent of thread locals for tasks. Note that the implications on data integrity in a distributed system apply also to sharing state between asynchronous components. Data races can occur on uncoordinated concurrent reads/writes of the shared state, which we explore in Chapter 7, "Synchronization Between Asyncio Components".

Sending Additional Information to an Asynchronous Generator

Problem

Asynchronous generators are very powerful features of the asyncio library and they enable us to reap the benefits of coroutine suspension, yielding intermediate values and sending values to the running asynchronous generator.

We learned how to do all this in our state machine example. Basically, the theory behind it is to iterate manually over the asynchronous generator, which is an arguably inelegant solution.

Focusing on the mechanism that is enabling the state machine, we will find a more generic solution to the problem in which we could also easily implement the state machine example.

Solution

We write an async context manager Python 3.7 style, using the
@asynccontextmanager decorator, and manually iterate it so we can send it
values while it runs.

```python
import asyncio
import logging
from contextlib import asynccontextmanager

class Interactor:
    def __init__(self, agen):
        self.agen = agen

    async def interact(self, *args, **kwargs, ):
        try:
            await self.agen.asend((args, kwargs))
        except StopAsyncIteration:
            logging.exception("The async generator is already
            exhausted!")

async def wrap_in_asyngen(handler):
    while True:
        args, kwargs = yield
        handler(*args, **kwargs)

@asynccontextmanager
async def start(agen):
    try:
        await agen.asend(None)
        yield Interactor(agen)
    finally:
        await agen.aclose()
```

```
async def main():
    async with start(wrap_in_asyngen(print)) as w:
        await w.interact("Put")
        await w.interact("the")
        await w.interact("worker")
        await w.interact("to")
        await w.interact("work!")

asyncio.run(main())
```

How It Works

The Interactor class encapsulates the part that enables the communication to the async generator. It uses the asend coroutine method to pass generic payloads, which it does by wrapping the *args and **kwargs parameters into a *tuple*.

Hence, the async generator needs to obey the contract and unwrap the payload. Our helper async generator wrap_in_asyngen passes these values to a callable that was passed via the handler parameter.

This helper async generator could behave state-fully, but mind you that the state of local variables will be resetted to the initial value if you yield them to the caller.

The start async context manager wraps the async generator in an Interactor and yields it back to us.

Calling interact calls asend under the hood, which is the equivalent of the async for loop behavior.

The async for loop first calls asend under the hood with None as an argument to initiate the iteration of the async generator.

Subsequent iteration steps call asend with None as an argument, until they receive the special sentinel value called _PyAsyncGenWrappedValue, which indicates to raise a StopAsyncIteration exception and contains the last yielded value.

If you control the asend calls manually, it is possible to push values to the asynchronous generator as demonstrated.

If you wanted to throw an exception into the asynchronous generator, you can also use the athrow coroutine for that. In that case, you would need to handle the exception inside the asynchronous generator function; otherwise, it will stop prematurely.

Using Queues with Coroutines

Problem

Queues are widely used for concurrency, especially in the context of multi-threaded or multi-process applications, so it's a very familiar process to developers.

If you want to migrate such an application to queues with coroutines, you might wonder if there is a similar data structure like the multiprocessing.Queue for asyncio that plays nice with coroutines.

Solution

Using asyncio.Queue, we can leverage asyncio-native objects to handle queuing of payloads.

```
import asyncio
import logging

logging.basicConfig(level=logging.DEBUG)

async def producer(iterable, queue: asyncio.Queue, shutdown_
event: asyncio.Event):
    for i in iterable:
```

```
            if shutdown_event.is_set():
                break
            try:
                queue.put_nowait(i)
                await asyncio.sleep(0)

            except asyncio.QueueFull as err:
                logging.warning("The queue is too full. Maybe the
                worker are too slow.")
                raise err

    shutdown_event.set()

async def worker(name, handler, queue: asyncio.Queue, shutdown_
event: asyncio.Event):
    while not shutdown_event.is_set() or not queue.empty():
        try:
            work = queue.get_nowait()
            # Simulate work
            handler(await asyncio.sleep(1.0, work))
            logging.debug(f"worker {name}: {work}")

        except asyncio.QueueEmpty:
            await asyncio.sleep(0)

async def main():
    n, handler, iterable = 10, lambda val: None, [i for i in
    range(500)]
    shutdown_event = asyncio.Event()
    queue = asyncio.Queue()
    worker_coros = [worker(f"worker_{i}", handler, queue,
    shutdown_event) for i in range(n)]
    producer_coro = producer(iterable, queue, shutdown_event)
```

```
coro = asyncio.gather(
    producer_coro,
    *worker_coros,
    return_exceptions=True
)
try:
    await  coro
except KeyboardInterrupt:
    shutdown_event.set()
    coro.cancel()
try:
    asyncio.run(main())
except KeyboardInterrupt:
    # It bubbles up
    logging.info("Pressed ctrl+c...")
```

How It Works

The worker-producer pattern works with coroutines as follows:

1. One producer coroutine produces new workloads that it puts into a queue for the worker coroutines to fetch.

2. It listens for the shutdown signal to stop producing new workloads and to gracefully shut down the program.

3. Using a queue, we must handle the asyncio. QueueFull exception. We set the shutdown_event from the producer when we have finished producing.

4. The worker coroutines, on the other hand, eagerly look for work in the queue and suspend if there is none. The indication for "no work" is a asyncio.QueueEmpty exception, while we have not received a shutdown event yet.

Note   It is important that we have an `async.sleep` somewhere in
the body of our worker so that other workers have a chance to grab
a workload too. It is also important to have an `async.sleep(0)`
inside the producer so that the workers have a chance to grab a
workload out of the queue. Otherwise, the workers will not start until
the producer has finished filling up the queue completely.

Communicating with a Subprocess Using Streams

The subprocesses API provides the means to spawn and entertain
subprocesses using underlying tools like fork and spawn in a more high-
level fashion.

Usually, we want to deploy IPC channels like pipes to talk to our
subprocess, but for multiple processes this method might get a bit clumsy.

Given that asyncio provides a nice asynchronous streaming API, we
will leverage it as a communication channel to our subprocesses.

Note that on a UNIX system, we recommend the second solution
using the UNIX server and connections that use UNIX *domain sockets*. The
benefits are that you can use the sophisticated UNIX *file permission system*
on your sockets for access control and benefit from speed improvements
since the IP stack mechanisms are bypassed.

To keep the argument parsing straightforward, we have decided to
separate these examples.

Solution #1: Windows and UNIX

Using the asyncio.start_server and asyncio.open_connection APIs, we
can have two subprocesses communicate with each other, besides using
pipes for IPC.

This example uses TCP sockets for communication and hence is
cross-platform.

```
import argparse
import asyncio
import sys

parser = argparse.ArgumentParser("streamserver")

subparsers = parser.add_subparsers(dest="command")
primary = subparsers.add_parser("primary")
secondary = subparsers.add_parser("secondary")
for subparser in (primary, secondary):
    subparser.add_argument("--host", default="127.0.0.1")
    subparser.add_argument("--port", default=1234)

async def connection_handler(reader: asyncio.StreamReader,
writer: asyncio.StreamWriter):
    print("Handler started")
    writer.write(b"Hi there!")
    await writer.drain()
    message = await reader.read(1024)
    print(message)

async def start_primary(host, port):
    await asyncio.create_subprocess_exec(sys.executable,
    __file__, "secondary", "--host", host, "--port",str(port),)
```

```
    server = await asyncio.start_server(connection_handler,
    host=host, port=port)
    async with server:
        await server.serve_forever()

async def start_secondary(host, port):
    reader, writer = await asyncio.open_connection(host, port)
    message = await reader.read(1024)
    print(message)
    writer.write(b"Hi yourself!")
    await writer.drain()
    writer.close()
    await writer.wait_closed()

async def main():
    args = parser.parse_args()

    if args.command == "primary":
        await start_primary(args.host, args.port)
    else:
        await start_secondary(args.host, args.port)

try:
    import logging
    logging.basicConfig(level=logging.DEBUG)
    logging.debug("Press ctrl+c to stop")
    if sys.platform == 'win32':
        asyncio.set_event_loop_policy(asyncio.
        WindowsProactorEventLoopPolicy())
    asyncio.run(main())
except KeyboardInterrupt:
    logging.debug("Stopped..")
```

Solution #2: UNIX Only

This example is UNIX only, since it uses UNIX domain sockets for communication.

To start the server, we use asyncio.start_unix_server and asyncio. open_unix_connection instead of the asyncio.start_server and asyncio.open_connection APIs.

```python
import argparse
import asyncio
import sys

parser = argparse.ArgumentParser("streamserver")

subparsers = parser.add_subparsers(dest="command")
primary = subparsers.add_parser("primary")
secondary = subparsers.add_parser("secondary")
for subparser in (primary, secondary):
    subparser.add_argument("--path", default="/tmp/asyncio.socket")

async def connection_handler(reader: asyncio.StreamReader,
writer: asyncio.StreamWriter):
    print("Handler started")
    writer.write(b"Hi there!")
    await writer.drain()
    message = await reader.read(1024)
    print(message)

async def start_primary(path):
    await asyncio.create_subprocess_exec(sys.executable,
    __file__, "secondary", "--path", path)
```

```python
    server = await asyncio.start_unix_server(connection_
    handler, path)
    async  with server:
        await server.serve_forever()

async def start_secondary(path):
    reader, writer = await asyncio.open_unix_connection(path)
    message = await reader.read(1024)
    print(message)
    writer.write(b"Hi yourself!")
    await writer.drain()
    writer.close()
    await writer.wait_closed()

async def main():
    args = parser.parse_args()

    if args.command == "primary":
        await start_primary(args.path)
    else:
        await start_secondary(args.path)
try:
    import logging
    logging.basicConfig(level=logging.DEBUG)
    logging.debug("Press ctrl+c to stop")
    asyncio.run(main())
except KeyboardInterrupt:
    logging.debug("Stopped..")
```

How It Works

This section applies to both solutions. The program can be started by invoking it in this fashion (on a UNIX system):

```
env python3 primary --host 127.0.0.1 --port <portnumber>
```

Or using this for the UNIX domain socket solution:

```
env python3 primary --path <path>
```

It will automatically spawn a child process using this:

```
await asyncio.create_subprocess_exec(sys.executable, __file__,
"secondary", "--host", host, "--port",str(port),)
```

or this for the UNIX domain socket solution:

```
await asyncio.create_subprocess_exec(sys.executable, __file__,
"secondary", "--path", path)
```

The following part is responsible for spawning the server and will call the connection_handler on every connection attempt. It will inject a StreamWriter and StreamReader instance:

```
server = await asyncio.start_unix_server(connection_handler, path)
async with server:
    await server.serve_forever()
```

The read API for the StreamReader is completely asynchronous and blocks until it there is actual data to read.

The writer API is not symmetrical, because the write* methods cannot be awaited.

Flow control has to be achieved via awaiting writer.drain, which blocks until the size of the buffer is drained down to the low watermark and writing can be resumed. It will immediately return if there is nothing to wait for.

To establish a connection to our stream server, we can use the following:

```
reader, writer = await asyncio.open_connection(host, port)
```

or use this for the UNIX domain socket solution:

```
reader, writer = await asyncio.open_unix_connection(path)
```

We receive stream readers and writers, which we can use to transfer payloads back and forth:

```
message = await reader.read(1024)
print(message)
writer.write(b"Hi yourself!")
await writer.drain()
writer.close()
await writer.wait_closed()
```

Note that we await `writer.wait_closed()` after the call to `writer.close()`, which is a new Python 3.7 API intended for this particular use. Note also that we don't need to close in the `StreamReader` case.

Writing a Simple RPC System with Asyncio

Using asyncio and MQTT as our transport layer, we can build a simple async RPC (remote procedure call) system.

Using RPC basically means that we can call a function/procedure defined in another program as if it belongs to our code. Choosing MQTT as a transport layer is best when we need to entertain a steady connection between the involved parties of our system in order to react to remote procedure calls between parties.

The parties involved are as follows:

- RPCRegistrar: The place where you register your remote procedures to signal availability to clients

- RPCClients: The consumers of remote procedures that were registered before

- RPCService: The provider of a remote procedure

This example assumes that you are running an instance of the Mosquitto MQTT server locally on the default port. It can be found for download here:

```
https://mosquitto.org/download/
```

Optionally, you can switch out the MQTT URL in the example with the official Mosquitto test server. See mqtt://test.mosquitto.org.

The example also assumes that you have installed the hbmqtt library. If you haven't installed it, you can do so via:

```
pip3 install hbmqtt
```

```
#or
```

```
pipenv install hbmqtt
```

Solution

Using the hbmqtt library, we can build an async MQTT binding for remote procedure calling. We will define a multi-stage protocol for invoking and getting the result of the call in a Pythonic way. MQTT works in a publish-subscribe fashion, which makes it perfect for interoperability with asyncio.Future.

```
import abc
import asyncio
import collections
```

```python
import inspect
import logging
import pickle
import typing
from contextlib import asynccontextmanager
from pickle import PickleError
from uuid import uuid4

from hbmqtt.client import MQTTClient, ConnectException
from hbmqtt.mqtt.constants import QOS_0

GET_REMOTE_METHOD = "get_remote_method"
GET_REMOTE_METHOD_RESPONSE = "get_remote_method/response"

CALL_REMOTE_METHOD = "call_remote_method"
CALL_REMOTE_METHOD_RESPONSE = "call_remote_method/response"

REGISTER_REMOTE_METHOD = "register_remote_method"
REGISTER_REMOTE_METHOD_RESPONSE = "register_remote_method/response"

logging.basicConfig(level=logging.INFO)

@asynccontextmanager
async def connect(url):
    client = MQTTClient()
    try:
        await client.connect(url)
        yield client
    except ConnectException:
        logging.exception(f"Could not connect to {url}")
    finally:
        await client.disconnect()
```

```python
@asynccontextmanager
async def pool(n, url):
    clients = [MQTTClient() for _ in range(n)]
    try:
        await asyncio.gather(*[client.connect(url) for client
        in clients])
        yield clients
    except ConnectException:
        logging.exception(f"Could not connect to {url}")
    finally:
        await asyncio.gather(*[client.disconnect() for client
        in clients])

def set_future_result(fut, result):
    if not fut:
        pass
    if isinstance(result, Exception):
        fut.set_exception(result)
    else:
        fut.set_result(result)

class RPCException(Exception):
    def __init__(self, message):
        self.message = message

    def __str__(self):
        return f"Error: {self.message}"

class RegisterRemoteMethodException(RPCException):
    def __init__(self):
        super(RegisterRemoteMethodException, self).__init__
        (f"Could not respond to {REGISTER_REMOTE_METHOD} query")
```

```python
class GetRemoteMethodException(RPCException):
    def __init__(self):
        super(GetRemoteMethodException, self).__init__(f"Could
        not respond to {GET_REMOTE_METHOD} query")

class CallRemoteMethodException(RPCException):
    def __init__(self):
        super(CallRemoteMethodException, self).__init__(f"Could
        not respond to {CALL_REMOTE_METHOD} query")

class RCPBase:

    def __init__(self, client: MQTTClient, topics: typing.
    List[str], qos=QOS_0):
        self.client = client
        self.running_fut = None
        self.topics = topics
        self.qos = qos

    @abc.abstractmethod
    async def on_get_remote_method(self, uuid_, service_name,
    function_name):
        raise NotImplementedError("Not implemented on_get_
        remote_method!")

    @abc.abstractmethod
    async def on_register_remote_method(self, uuid_, service_
    name, function_name, signature):
        raise NotImplementedError("Not implemented on_register_
        remote_method!")

    @abc.abstractmethod
    async def on_call_remote_method(self, uuid_, service_name,
    function_name, args, kwargs):
```

```
    raise NotImplementedError("Not implemented on_call_
    remote_method!")

@abc.abstractmethod
async def on_get_remote_method_response(self, uuid_,
service_name, function_name, signature_or_exception):
    raise NotImplementedError("Not implemented on_get_
    remote_method_response!")

@abc.abstractmethod
async def on_register_remote_method_response(self, uuid_,
service_name, function_name, is_registered_or_exception):
    raise NotImplementedError("Not implemented on_register_
    remote_method_response!")

@abc.abstractmethod
async def on_call_remote_method_response(self, uuid_,
service_name, function_name, result_or_exception):
    raise NotImplementedError("Not implemented on_call_
    remote_method_response!")

async def next_message(self):
    message = await self.client.deliver_message()
    packet = message.publish_packet
    topic_name, payload = packet.variable_header.topic_
    name, packet.payload.data
    return topic_name, payload

async def loop(self):
    while True:
        topic, payload = await self.next_message()
        try:
            yield topic, pickle.loads(payload)
```

```python
        except (PickleError, AttributeError, EOFError,
        ImportError, IndexError):
            logging.exception("Could not deserialize
            payload: %s for topic: %s", payload, topic)

async def __aenter__(self):
    self.running_fut = asyncio.ensure_future(self.start())
    await self.client.subscribe([
        (topic, self.qos) for topic in self.topics
    ])
    return self

async def __aexit__(self, exc_type, exc_val, exc_tb):
    await self.stop()
    await self.client.unsubscribe(self.topics)

async def start(self):
    async for topic, payload in self.loop():
        try:
            if topic == REGISTER_REMOTE_METHOD:
                await self.on_register_remote_
                method(*payload)
            elif topic == GET_REMOTE_METHOD:
                await self.on_get_remote_method(*payload)
            elif topic == CALL_REMOTE_METHOD:
                await self.on_call_remote_method(*payload)
            elif topic == REGISTER_REMOTE_METHOD_RESPONSE:
                await self.on_register_remote_method_
                response(*payload)
            elif topic == GET_REMOTE_METHOD_RESPONSE:
                await self.on_get_remote_method_
                response(*payload)
            elif topic == CALL_REMOTE_METHOD_RESPONSE:
```

```
                await self.on_call_remote_method_
                response(*payload)
            except TypeError:
                logging.exception(f"Could not call handler for
                topic: %s and payload: %s", topic, payload)
            except NotImplementedError:
                pass

    async def stop(self):
        if self.running_fut:
            self.running_fut.cancel()

    async def wait(self):
        if self.running_fut:
            await asyncio.shield(self.running_fut)

class RemoteMethod:

    def __init__(self, rpc_client, signature, function_name,
    qos=QOS_0):
        self.rpc_client = rpc_client
        self.signature = signature
        self.function_name = function_name
        self.qos = qos

    async def __call__(self, *args, **kwargs, ):
        uuid_ = str(uuid4())
        service_name = self.rpc_client.service_name
        payload = (uuid_, service_name, self.function_name,
        args, kwargs)
        fut = asyncio.Future()
        self.rpc_client.call_remote_method_requests.
        setdefault(service_name, {}).setdefault(self.function_
        name, {})[
            uuid_] = fut
```

```python
        await self.rpc_client.client.publish(CALL_REMOTE_METHOD,
        pickle.dumps(payload), qos=self.qos)
        return await fut

class RPCClient(RCPBase):
    def __init__(self, client, service_name, topics=None,
    qos=QOS_0):
        if not topics:
            topics = [CALL_REMOTE_METHOD_RESPONSE, GET_REMOTE_
            METHOD_RESPONSE, ]
        super(RPCClient, self).__init__(client, topics, qos=qos)
        self.call_remote_method_requests = collections.
        defaultdict(dict)
        self.get_remote_method_requests = collections.
        defaultdict(dict)
        self.list_remote_methods_requests = collections.
        defaultdict(dict)
        self.responses = collections.defaultdict(dict)
        self.service_name = service_name
        self.remote_methods_cache = collections.defaultdict(dict)

    def __getattr__(self, item):
        return asyncio.ensure_future(self.get_remote_method(item))

    async def get_remote_method(self, function_name):
        while True:
            uuid_ = str(uuid4())
            payload = (uuid_, self.service_name, function_name)
            fut = asyncio.Future()
            self.get_remote_method_requests.setdefault(self.
            service_name, {}).setdefault(function_name, {})[uuid_] = fut
```

```
        await self.client.publish(GET_REMOTE_METHOD, pickle.
        dumps(payload), qos=QOS_0)
        # Might throw GetRemoteMethodException
        try:
            signature = await asyncio.shield(fut)
            return RemoteMethod(self, signature, function_
            name)
        except GetRemoteMethodException:
            await asyncio.sleep(0)

    async def on_call_remote_method_response(self, uuid_, service_
    name, function_name, result_or_exception):
        fut = self.call_remote_method_requests.get(service_name,
        {}).get(function_name, {}).pop(uuid_, None)
        set_future_result(fut, result_or_exception)

    async def on_get_remote_method_response(self, uuid_, service_
    name, function_name, signature_or_exception):
        fut = self.get_remote_method_requests.get(service_name,
        {}).get(function_name, {}).pop(uuid_, None)
        set_future_result(fut, signature_or_exception)

class RPCService(RCPBase):
    def __init__(self, client: MQTTClient, name: str, topics:
    typing.List[str] = None, qos=QOS_0):
        if not topics:
            topics = [REGISTER_REMOTE_METHOD_RESPONSE, CALL_
            REMOTE_METHOD]
        super(RPCService, self).__init__(client, topics, qos=qos)
        self.name = name
        self.client = client
        self.qos = qos
```

```
        self.register_remote_method_requests = collections.
        defaultdict(dict)
        self.remote_methods = collections.defaultdict(dict)

    async def register_function(self, remote_function):
        function_name = remote_function.__name__
        uuid_ = str(uuid4())
        payload = pickle.dumps((uuid_, self.name, function_name,
        inspect.signature(remote_function)))
        fut = asyncio.Future()
        self.register_remote_method_requests.setdefault(self.name,
        {}).setdefault(function_name, {})[uuid_] = fut
        self.remote_methods[self.name][function_name] = remote_
        function
        await self.client.publish(REGISTER_REMOTE_METHOD, payload,
        qos=self.qos)
        return await asyncio.shield(fut)

    async def on_register_remote_method_response(self, uuid_,
    service_name, function_name, is_registered_or_exception):
        fut = self.register_remote_method_requests.get(service_
        name, {}).get(function_name, {}).get(uuid_, None)
        set_future_result(fut, is_registered_or_exception)

    async def on_call_remote_method(self, uuid_, service_name,
    function_name, args, kwargs):
        remote_method = self.remote_methods.get(service_name, {}).
        get(function_name, None)
        if not remote_method:
            payload = pickle.dumps((uuid_, service_name, function_
            name, CallRemoteMethodException()))
            return await self.client.publish(CALL_REMOTE_METHOD_
            RESPONSE, payload, qos=self.qos)
```

```python
        try:
            result = await remote_method(*args, **kwargs)
            payload = pickle.dumps((uuid_, service_name, function_
            name, result))
            return await self.client.publish(CALL_REMOTE_METHOD_
            RESPONSE, payload, qos=self.qos)
        except Exception as err:
            payload = pickle.dumps((uuid_, service_name, function_
            name, err))
            return await self.client.publish(CALL_REMOTE_METHOD_
            RESPONSE, payload, qos=self.qos)

class RemoteRegistrar(RCPBase):
    def __init__(self, client: MQTTClient, topics: typing.
    List[str] = None, qos=QOS_0):
        if not topics:
            topics = [REGISTER_REMOTE_METHOD, GET_REMOTE_METHOD]
        super(RemoteRegistrar, self).__init__(client, topics,
        qos=qos)
        self.registrar = collections.defaultdict(dict)

    async def on_register_remote_method(self, uuid_, service_name,
    function_name, signature):
        try:
            self.registrar.setdefault(service_name, {})[function_
            name] = signature
            payload = pickle.dumps((uuid_, service_name, function_
            name, True), )
            await self.client.publish(REGISTER_REMOTE_METHOD_
            RESPONSE, payload)
```

```
        except Exception:
            # A broad exception clause like this is bad practice
            but we are only interested in the outcome of saving
            the signature, so we convert it
            logging.exception(f"Failed to save signature: {signature}")
            payload = pickle.dumps((uuid_, service_name, function_
            name, RegisterRemoteMethodException()))
            await self.client.publish(REGISTER_REMOTE_METHOD_
            RESPONSE, payload, )

    async def on_get_remote_method(self, uuid_, service_name,
    function_name):
        signature = self.registrar.get(service_name, {}).
        get(function_name, None)

        if signature:
            payload = pickle.dumps((uuid_, service_name, function_
            name, signature), )
            await self.client.publish(GET_REMOTE_METHOD_RESPONSE,
            payload)
        else:
            payload = pickle.dumps((uuid_, service_name, function_
            name, GetRemoteMethodException()), )
            await self.client.publish(GET_REMOTE_METHOD_RESPONSE,
            payload)

async def remote_function(i: int, f: float, s: str):
    print("It worked")
    return f

async def register_with_delay(rpc_service, remote_function,
delay=3):
    await asyncio.sleep(delay)
    await rpc_service.register_function(remote_function)
```

```python
async def main(url="mqtt://localhost", service_name="TestService"):
    async with pool(3, url) as (client, client1, client2):
        async with RemoteRegistrar(client):
            async with RPCService(client1, service_name) as rpc_
            service:
                async with RPCClient(client2, service_name) as
                rpc_client:
                    asyncio.ensure_future(register_with_delay(rpc_
                    service, remote_function))
                    handler = await asyncio.wait_for(rpc_client.
                    remote_function,timeout=10)
                    res = await handler(1, 3.4, "")
                    print(res)

if __name__ == '__main__':
    asyncio.run(main())
```

How It Works

MQTT uses so-called *topics,* which you can send payloads to and subscribe on.

We use three topics and their respective "response" topics to facilitate our RPC bus. They are defined as follows:

```python
GET_REMOTE_METHOD = "get_remote_method"
GET_REMOTE_METHOD_RESPONSE = "get_remote_method/response"

CALL_REMOTE_METHOD = "call_remote_method"
CALL_REMOTE_METHOD_RESPONSE = "call_remote_method/response"

REGISTER_REMOTE_METHOD = "register_remote_method"
REGISTER_REMOTE_METHOD_RESPONSE = "register_remote_method/response"
```

We implement our own simple message ID on MQTT using its least reliable modus operandi in terms of quality of service, which means that every message is sent at most once, with no acknowledgment message.

For convenience, we define async context managers for MQTTClient that handle the disconnections and a pool that creates multiple MQTTClient instances.

```
@asynccontextmanager
async def connect(url):
        # snip ..

@asynccontextmanager
async def pool(n, url):
    # snip ..
```

We will use the pool in this example because the MQTTClient instance cannot be shared across our three aforementioned parties. We will invoke the whole machinery in one process for ease of demonstration. (Ideally, we should have three separate processes and hence three instances.)

We define a helper function that we use to interact with futures hassle-free. If we pass it a non-exception value, we want it to be set as such; otherwise, we call set exception. We need to do this because we are listening to MQTT messages on their respective (non-async) loops. When we find a message to a topic that our party has subscribed to, we check if the IDs of the message and the stored future match and use this helper to wake the party from awaiting the future.

We also define a couple of exceptions that are thrown when something goes wrong on the respective topics.

```
def set_future_result(fut, result):
    if not fut:
        pass
    if isinstance(result, Exception):
        fut.set_exception(result)
```

```
    else:
        fut.set_result(result)

class RPCException(Exception):
    # snip...

class RegisterRemoteMethodException(RPCException):
    # snip...

class GetRemoteMethodException(RPCException):
    # snip...

class CallRemoteMethodException(RPCException):
    # snip...
```

Next, we define the RCPBase class, which defines an interface to be implemented by parties that want to define callbacks to the respective topics.

It can be passed topics that it will unsubscribe/subscribe upon entering/exiting if it is used as an async context manager.

Furthermore, it will take care of starting its message loop and calling the correct callbacks.

By awaiting its wait method, we can block indefinitely. This is useful for the RPCRegistrar and the RPCService.

The RemoteMethod class abstracts away a method belonging to a remote service. Note that __call__ is a coroutine (!) and it takes care of publishing the *args and **kwargs parameters to the CALL_REMOTE_METHOD topic, using pickle as a serializing mechanism.

```
class RemoteMethod:
    # snip ..
```

The RPCClient starts with the service name set to the name of the RPCService instance that we are interested in.

We override the __getattr__ to schedule a get_remote_method call, which in turn returns a future we can await. It returns if the remote method was registered and turns into a RemoteMethod. It will block indefinitely if this doesn't happen, so we await it with a timeout.

We use the RPCService to register a function. It publishes the intent on the respective topic that the registrar is listening to when calling its register_function coroutine method.

The communication happens on the topic and its corresponding <topicname>/response channel where the subscribing party answers.

The registrar saves the serialized signature object of the respective function, which could, for instance, be used for parameter validation.

The main coroutine is straightforward. It shows the delayed registration of a function that we embedded to demonstrate that you could very well use these components in different processes/call order.

```python
async def main(url="mqtt://localhost", service_
name="TestService"):
    async with pool(3, url) as (client, client1, client2):
        async with RemoteRegistrar(client):
            async with RPCService(client1, service_name) as
            rpc_service:
                async with RPCClient(client2, service_name) as
                rpc_client:
                    asyncio.ensure_future(register_with_
                    delay(rpc_service, remote_function))
                    handler = await asyncio.wait_for(rpc_
                    client.remote_function,timeout=10)
                    res = await handler(1, 3.4, "")
                    print(res)
```

Writing Callbacks that Have a "Memory" Using Contextvars

Sometimes it is nice to have "coroutine-local" context that can be shared across runs, but is private inside the run. This basically means that two coroutines that access the same key should have their private version/view on their context variable.

Fortunately, PEP 567 introduced such a concept through the contextvars module.

It provides three new APIs that can be used from the world of asyncio:

- ContextVar

- Context

- Token

Solution #1

We demonstrate that ContextVar instances are indeed coroutine-local by constructing an example with multiple accesses to the value stored in the same key from different coroutines.

```
import contextvars
from contextvars import ContextVar
import asyncio

context = contextvars.copy_context()
context_var = ContextVar('key', default=None)

async def memory(context_var, value):
    old_value = context_var.get()
    context_var.set(value)
    print(old_value, value)
```

```
async def main():
    await asyncio.gather(*[memory(context_var, i) for i in
    range(10)])

asyncio.run(main())
```

How It Works

Using `context` = `contextvars.copy_context()`, we get a copy of the current Context object which is a "[..] new generic mechanism of ensuring consistent access to non-local state in the context of out-of-order execution [..]" (Source: `https://www.python.org/dev/peps/pep-0550/`) for the current OS thread, which is just shallow. So, the caller is the sole owner of the Context object.

The ContextVar must be defined outside of a function scope and is used for a lookup on the "current" coroutine-local context object by passing itself as a key.

By calling memory simultaneously multiple times, we can see that the access to `context_var` is indeed coroutine-local, since it always starts with the default value.

Solution #2

We demonstrate how synchronous callbacks use ContextVar instances for context awareness.

```
import contextvars
import functools
from contextvars import ContextVar

context = contextvars.copy_context()
context_var = ContextVar('key', default=None)

def resetter(context_var, token, invalid_values):
```

```
    value = context_var.get()
    if value in invalid_values:
        context_var.reset(token)

def blacklist(context_var, value, resetter):
    old_value = context_var.get()
    token = context_var.set(value)
    resetter(context_var, token)
    print(old_value)

for i in range(10):
    context.run(blacklist, context_var, i, functools.
    partial(resetter, invalid_values=[5, 6, 7, 8, 9]))
```

How It Works

Synchronous callbacks can also benefit from context-aware storage.
By using context.run, we can ensure that the context is not accessed
from more than one OS thread. This is because context.run raises a
RuntimeError when it's called on the same context object from more than
one OS thread, or when it's called recursively.

We also learned about the Token API, which can be used to reset
the context to a previously set value. Tokens are returned by invoking a
ContextVar.set method. To return to a previous state given by a token
object, we invoke ContextVar.reset(token).

CHAPTER 7

Synchronization Between Asyncio Components

Asyncio enables us to write cooperative concurrent systems. There are no mechanisms to ensure their correctness in terms of *safety* and *liveness*. *Safety* in this context means to remain in an "intended" state and not divert from it. *Liveness* in this context means to "make progress," basically that the intended states of the program are reached.

A program consists of critical and uncritical paths of execution. A critical path is characterized by the access of a shared resource. Synchronization in our context means that we ensure mutually exclusive access of the shared resource for one coroutine. Ironically, claiming exclusive control over a shared resource inside a critical path is one of the Coffman conditions. We need to be careful to not run into deadlocks while trying to fix our synchronization problems.

It's the responsibility of the developer to ensure that the code demonstrates named properties. We want to narrow down our understanding of safety in the realm of concurrency for asyncio to a very practical one:

The (critical) paths of our application allow access of shared data; allow one coroutine exclusively to access the shared data from the coroutine's beginning until the coroutine's ending.

© Mohamed Mustapha Tahrioui 2019
M. M. Tahrioui, *asyncio Recipes*, https://doi.org/10.1007/978-1-4842-4401-2_7

To ensure the liveness of the asyncio program, we need to ensure we do not construct code that runs into a deadlock. A *deadlock* can be understood as a situation in time where the system fulfills the four Coffman conditions simultaneously:

- Tasks claim exclusive control of the resources they require (the *mutual exclusion* condition).

- Tasks hold resources already allocated to them while waiting for additional resources (the *wait for* condition).

- Resources cannot be forcibly removed from the tasks holding them until the resources are used to completion (the *no preemption* condition).

- A circular chain of tasks exists, such that each task holds one or more resources that are being requested by the next task in the chain (the *circular wait* condition).

Note   These are necessary but not sufficient conditions for a deadlock. Removing them however is sufficient to not have deadlock, i.e., to ensure the liveness of the program.

Using Locks for Mutual Exclusive Access to a Shared Resource

Problem

You want to provide mutual exclusive access to coroutines concerning a shared resource.

Solution

Using knowledge about async context managers, we can use asyncio.Lock on context exclusively for one coroutine to access some resource:

```
import asyncio

NON_ATOMIC_SUM_KEY = 'non_atomic_sum'
ATOMIC_SUM_KEY = 'atomic_sum'
DATABASE = {ATOMIC_SUM_KEY: 0, NON_ATOMIC_SUM_KEY: 0}

async def add_with_delay(key, value, delay):
    old_value = DATABASE[key]
    await asyncio.sleep(delay)
    DATABASE[key] = old_value + value

async def add_locked_with_delay(lock, key, value, delay):
    async with lock:
        old_value = DATABASE[key]
        await asyncio.sleep(delay)
        DATABASE[key] = old_value + value

async def main():
    # An asyncio lock can be used to guarantee exclusive access
    to a shared resource
    lock = asyncio.Lock()
    atomic_workers = [
        add_locked_with_delay(lock, ATOMIC_SUM_KEY, 1, 3),
        add_locked_with_delay(lock, ATOMIC_SUM_KEY, 1, 2),
    ]
    non_atomic_workers = [
        add_with_delay(NON_ATOMIC_SUM_KEY, 1, 3),
        add_with_delay(NON_ATOMIC_SUM_KEY, 1, 2),
    ]
```

```
    await asyncio.gather(*non_atomic_workers)
    await asyncio.gather(*atomic_workers)

    assert DATABASE.get(ATOMIC_SUM_KEY) == 2
    assert DATABASE.get(NON_ATOMIC_SUM_KEY) != 2

asyncio.run(main())
```

How It Works

The CPython interpreter has a global lock that influences the interpreter's process parallelism. Only one native thread can effectively operate at a time, meaning executing bytecode. This means since asyncio, we have three ways in Python to run into synchronization issues/data races:

- Threaded code that gets non-cooperatively preempted (suspended)

- Multi-process code

- Asyncio code that yields control back to the event loop via `await asyncio.sleep(n)` inside the critical path that accesses the shared memory

Asyncio gets interfaces for coroutines (event loops and the `async def` keyword), multiprocessing (using subprocesses), and to threads (using the event loop's executor API).

In asyncio, the `asyncio.Lock` async context manager is the correct way to provide mutual exclusive access to a shared resource.

Note   Using the lock interface directly by awaiting the `acquire` and `release` coroutine methods is considered deprecated! The threading module and the multiprocessing module provide their version of a lock context manager to ensure mutual exclusive access to shared resources for threads and processes.

The asyncio version allows only one coroutine to enter its scope. We compare access to a data race and one without and see how the lock came into the picture to enable a data-race-free access.

Note   Every access to a resource must happen under the same lock to ensure data-race freeness. If you enter the async context manager lock's scope, it will call `acquire` in its __aenter__ hook for you.

This call blocks until all the other parties that tried to call `acquire` have returned. To signal to the lock that it is free again, the `release` coroutine method is called in __aexit__ by the lock. This will ensure that the first waiter in the dequeue is notified. This way, only one coroutine is "inside" the lock's context at any time.

In our example, we construct two coroutine functions—add_with_delay and add_locked_with_delay. They access a dictionary value via the same key, suspend themselves with `asyncio.sleep,` and write the initial value they have read into the dictionary while adding a value they were passed as a parameter.

They differ in their behavior based on how they behave in this critical path. add_with_delay does not bother about synchronization and dd_locked_with_delay locks the whole critical path up. This way, only one coroutine can access the dictionary at the same time in reading and writing.

Note   The interesting bit here is that the presence of the lock indicates that the context switch is useless. We could also have chosen a more elaborate example—splitting, getting, and adding the value into two coroutines—but we chose not to, since both examples demonstrate the same principle.

Using Events for Notification

Problem

You want to notify waiting tasks that an event they are waiting on has occurred.

Solution

asyncio events are intended to signal to multiple coroutines, hence the coroutine method can be reused and will block until the event is "set". We demonstrate how a (service) cleanup pattern could be built using an event loop.

```python
import asyncio
import logging
import random

logging.basicConfig(level=logging.INFO)

async def busy_loop(interval, work, worker, shutdown_event):
    while not shutdown_event.is_set():
        await worker(work)
        await asyncio.sleep(interval)
    logging.info("Shutdown event was set..")
    return work

async def cleanup(mess, shutdown_event):
    await shutdown_event.wait()
    logging.info("Cleaning up the mess: %s...", mess)
    # Add cleanup logic here

async def shutdown(delay, shutdown_event):
    await asyncio.sleep(delay)
    shutdown_event.set()
```

```python
async def add_mess(mess_pile, ):
    mess = random.randint(1, 10)
    logging.info("Adding the mess: %s...", mess)
    mess_pile.append(mess)

async def main():
    shutdown_event = asyncio.Event()
    shutdown_delay = 10
    work = []
    await asyncio.gather(*[
        shutdown(shutdown_delay, shutdown_event),
        cleanup(work, shutdown_event),
        busy_loop(1, work, add_mess, shutdown_event),
    ])

asyncio.run(main())
```

How It Works

We await three coroutines in our main method:

- `shutdown(shutdown_delay, shutdown_event)`
- `cleanup(work, shutdown_event)`
- `busy_loop(1, work, add_mess, shutdown_event)`

Shutdown is a helper coroutine method that "sets" the event instance we pass to all coroutines. In other words, it notifies all coroutines currently waiting or checking its status via event.is_set that it's finished. Since the busy_loop needs to perform work periodically, it doesn't make sense for it to await the event signal, so it's polling it via event.is_set before starting to invoke the worker. The cleanup coroutine, on the other hand, demonstrates how you wait for the event to be set by awaiting its event. wait() coroutine.

153

Using Condition Variables for Control Flow

Problem

You want to grant mutually exclusive access to a shared resource.

Solution

Condition variables were introduced in a prior chapter, but not as a synchronization mechanism. Basically, condition variables can be best understood as locks coupled with event variables. The following example shows us to build a stock watcher given multiple condition variables the share one lock instance:

```python
import asyncio
import random

STOCK_MARKET = {
    "DAX": 100,
    "SPR": 10,
    "AMAZON": 1000,
}

INITIAL_STOCK_MARKET = STOCK_MARKET.copy()

class MarketException(BaseException):
    pass

async def stock_watcher(on_alert, stock, price, cond):
    async with cond:
        print(f"Waiting for {stock} to be under {price}$")
        await cond.wait_for(lambda: STOCK_MARKET.get(stock) <
        price)
        await on_alert()
```

```python
def random_stock():
    while True:
        yield random.choice(list(STOCK_MARKET.keys()))

async def twitter_quotes(conds, threshold):
    for stock in random_stock():
        STOCK_MARKET[stock] -= random.randint(1, 10)
        new_value = STOCK_MARKET[stock]
        print(f"New stock market value for {stock}: {new_value}")
        if new_value < threshold:
            cond = conds.get(stock)
            async with cond:
                cond.notify()
        await asyncio.sleep(.1)

async def governmental_market_surveillance():
    raise MarketException()

async def main():
    lock = asyncio.Lock()
    conditions = {stock: asyncio.Condition(lock) for stock in
    STOCK_MARKET}
    threshold = -50
    stock_watchers = [
        stock_watcher(
            governmental_market_surveillance,
            stock,
            threshold,
            conditions.get(stock)
        ) for stock in STOCK_MARKET
    ]
```

```
    await asyncio.gather(*[twitter_quotes(conditions, threshold),
    *stock_watchers], return_exceptions=False)
try:
    asyncio.run(main())
except MarketException:
    print("Restoring the stock market..")
    STOCK_MARKET = INITIAL_STOCK_MARKET.copy()
```

How It Works

The solution demonstrates how we can await dynamically calculated conditions. We create a `stock_watcher` instance for each stock and pass it a condition variable that has an instance of the same lock.

Using the same lock is important, otherwise awaiting `condition.wait_for` will block indefinitely! The `acquire`, `release`, and `locked` methods of the condition variable are just pass-throughs of the lock methods. If you don't use the same lock, the coroutines will not be governed by the same context and in consequence not synchronized.

`condition.wait_for` is passed a callable. As long as the callable returns a false value awaiting, the `condition.wait_for` coroutine will block. Nonetheless, the condition variable needs to be signaled as to when to check for the condition using `cond.notify`.

To call the method, we need to acquire the lock first by using the async context manager protocol on the condition variable:

```
async with cond:
    cond.notify()
```

Note   This check is redundant: `if new_value < threshold:`. It can be removed, since we use `cond.wait_for` and not `cond. wait`. The context switch after invoking `cond.notify` via `await asyncio.sleep(.1)` is necessary since it gives the condition variable the chance to check if the condition became true.

The delay is not important as long it is bigger than or equal to zero. Equal to zero would skip exactly one loop iteration.

Using Semaphores to Restrict Concurrent Resource Access

Problem

You want to allow only a limited number of coroutines operating in a context.

Solution

We see how to have 10 concurrent workers at most using `asyncio.` Semaphores in this example:

```
import asyncio

async def run(i, semaphore):
    async with semaphore:
        print(f"{i} working..")
        return await asyncio.sleep(1)
```

```
async def main():
    semaphore = asyncio.Semaphore(10)
    await asyncio.gather(*[run(i, semaphore) for i in
    range(100)])

asyncio.run(main())
```

How It Works

Semaphores operate like locks in the sense that they allow only a limited number of coroutines operating in their context (they are implemented as async context managers as well). This way, we can implement techniques like paging or restrict simultaneous connections quite easily.

We can restrict simultaneous connections quite easily by adding a semaphore to the async with clause like this:

```
async with semaphore, connect as connection:
    # continue...
```

Semaphores entertain a dequeue of "waiters". They let the dequeue fill up until they hit their cap. If one of the currently executing coroutine finishes and drops out of the context scope, __aexit__ will wake the next waiter if there is one. This way, we always have a maximum of 10 workers operating at the same time.

Note   Using the semaphore interface directly by awaiting the acquire and release coroutine methods is considered deprecated!

Using Bounded Semaphores to Restrict Concurrent Resource Access with Stricter Release Heuristics

Problem

We want to use a drop-in replacement for asyncio.Semaphore with a stricter release heuristic.

Solution

Bounded semaphores are the same as semaphores, but have an additional sanity check in their release method:

```
def release(self):
    if self._value >= self._bound_value:
        raise ValueError('BoundedSemaphore released too many
        times')
    super().release()
```

Note   Since it is discouraged to use the acquire and release methods directly, this situation is highly unlikely to happen unless you tamper with the value manually.

We see how to have a maximum of 10 concurrent workers using asyncio.BoundedSemaphores in this example:

```
import asyncio

async def run(i, semaphore):
    async with semaphore:
```

```
        print(f"{i} working..")
        return await asyncio.sleep(1)
async def main():
    semaphore = asyncio.BoundedSemaphore(10)
    await asyncio.gather(*[run(i, semaphore) for i in
    range(100)])

asyncio.run(main(),debug=True)
```

How It Works

We demonstrated that the asyncio.BoundedSemaphore can be used as a
drop-in replacement for asyncio.Semaphore for our purposes, since it is
actually inheriting from it and simply adds a sanity check to the release
method.

Detecting Asyncio Code That Might Have Race Conditions

Problem

Given the prelude about race conditions and possible race condition
vectors in asyncio applications, we want to understand where exactly the
data race happens in our application.

Solution #1

This solution provides a reproducible case of a data race—much like the
one we saw in this chapter—where we can annotate exactly where the data
race happens.

```python
import asyncio
import typing

async def delayed_add(delay, d: typing.Dict, key: typing.
Hashable, value: float):
    last = d[key] # This is where the critical path starts, d
    is the shared resource and this is a read access
    await asyncio.sleep(delay)
    d[key] = last + value # This is where the critical path
    ends, d is the shared resource and this is a write access

async def main():
    d = {"value": 0}
    await asyncio.gather(delayed_add(2, d, "value", 1.0),
    delayed_add(1.0, d, "value", 1.0))
    print(d)
    assert d["value"] != 2

asyncio.run(main())
```

How It Works

This case falls under the category of coroutine data races induced by context switches (asyncio.sleep). We have touched upon the fact that our example with delayed_add was designed for educational value rather than being a realistic example. The reason it's not realistic is evident in the critical path of the application. There is no chaining of coroutines involved, so we can easily see where the access to the shared resource happens.

Strong indicators for a possible asyncio race condition is the use of asyncio.sleep.

Using asyncio.sleep destroys the invariant that the (coroutine) function body is executed completely.

This means that other coroutines could alter the resources accessed by the first coroutine.

In other words, asyncio.sleep has the potential to render access to a shared resource non-exclusively, corresponding to the first Coffman condition.

Thus, it is imperative to inspect all coroutine functions/methods that have context switches using asyncio.sleep and follow all the calls to asyncio.ensure_future, asyncio.create_task, loop.create_task, and uses of the await keyword for interactions with your shared resources.

Solution #2

The next example demonstrates a data race case involving the loop's executor API in conjunction with the ThreadPoolExecutor.

```python
import asyncio
import threading
import time
from concurrent.futures.thread import ThreadPoolExecutor

def add_from_thread(delay, d, key, value):
    print(f"Thread {threading.get_ident()} started...")
    old = d[key]
    print(f"Thread {threading.get_ident()} read value {old}")
    time.sleep(delay)
    print(f"Thread {threading.get_ident()} slept for {delay}
    seconds")
    d[key] = old + value
    print(f"Thread {threading.get_ident()} wrote {d[key]}")

async def main():
    loop = asyncio.get_running_loop()
    d = {"value": 0}
```

```
    executor = ThreadPoolExecutor(10)
    futs = [loop.run_in_executor(executor, add_from_thread, 1,
    d, "value", 1),
            loop.run_in_executor(executor, add_from_thread, 3,
            d, "value", 1)]
    await asyncio.gather(*futs)

    assert d["value"] != 2

asyncio.run(main())
```

How It Works

This case falls under the category of thread data races induced by the executor API. Threads are governed by non-cooperative preemption. This means that the scheduler (OS, in the case of native threads) decides when to suspend the thread.

Additionally, preemption might happen if we call time.sleep inside the thread. An easy way to see if we have two agents simultaneously accessing the same shared resource (dictionary "d") is to add print statements with the current thread identifier and the currently executed operation.

Note   The overhead of the print operation might skew the results of our observations since it deploys global locking.

In this case, we can clearly see that the threads access the shared resource in an intervened, race-prone way:

```
Thread 123145539575808 started...
Thread 123145539575808 read value 0
Thread 123145544830976 started...
```

```
Thread 123145544830976 read value 0
Thread 123145539575808 slept for 1
Thread 123145539575808 wrote 1
Thread 123145544830976 slept for 3
Thread 123145544830976 wrote 1
```

Both threads start reading the value before one thread can successfully read *and* write it to the dictionary. Thus, the initial value 0 was used both places to write to the dictionary instead of 1 (in the case of a successful read sequential, write).

In a completely sequential example, we would assume the result of the computation is 2, whereas in this case it is 1.

## CHAPTER 8

Improving Asyncio Applications

To be able to determine if we have improved the code quality of our asyncio code, we must come to common terms about which parts of the code concern us. One universal, non-functional measure of code quality that we will apply is memory and time consumption of code. The other measure used in this chapter is to avoid using APIs that have been deprecated.

To do that, the sections of this chapter illustrate how to build and use profiling tools to measure the allocated memory and duration of coroutines. Also, we learn which asyncio patterns have been deprecated and build a tool that uses the ast module to automatically recognize them. In the last example, we learn about an anti-pattern called *busy loops* and how to avoid it using future objects.

Profiling Asyncio Applications

Problem

You are concerned about the memory and time used by an application in the course of a coroutine call.

© Mohamed Mustapha Tahrioui 2019
M. M. Tahrioui, *asyncio Recipes*, https://doi.org/10.1007/978-1-4842-4401-2_8

Solution

Profiling in this context is measuring non-functional parameters of program execution. To do this, the Python standard library includes the `tracemalloc` module outlined in PEP 454. The `tracemalloc` module was introduced in the CPython interpreter due to a need for a Python-specific memory monitoring API. Memory management in CPython is handled by two APIs— `PyMem_Malloc` and `pymalloc`. These allocators don't play well with generic memory debuggers like `Valgrind`, which can give you the C traceback to your allocations, which would result in tracebacks ending in CPython C APIs like `PyMem_Malloc` and `pymalloc`. We use the `tracemalloc` module and a `profiler` class with a decorator to print our coroutine's memory usage.

```python
import asyncio
import logging
import tracemalloc
from functools import wraps

logging.basicConfig(level=logging.DEBUG)

class Profiler:
    def __init__(self):
        self.stats = {}
        self.logger = logging.getLogger(__name__)

    def profile_memory_usage(self, f):
        @wraps(f)
        async def wrapper(*args, **kwargs):
            snapshot = tracemalloc.take_snapshot()
            res = await f(*args, **kwargs)
            self.stats[f.__name__] = tracemalloc.take_
            snapshot().compare_to(snapshot, 'lineno')
            return res

        return wrapper
```

```python
    def print(self):
        for name, stats in self.stats.items():
            for entry in stats:
                self.logger.debug(entry)

    def __enter__(self):
        tracemalloc.start()
        return self

    def __exit__(self, exc_type, exc_val, exc_tb):
        tracemalloc.stop()
        self.print()

profiler = Profiler()

@profiler.profile_memory_usage
async def main():
    pass

with profiler:
    asyncio.run(main())
```

How It Works

The profiler class is used as a container for the coroutine function-
related memory statistics. For this purpose, it defines a stats attribute in
its __init__ method:

```python
class Profiler:
    def __init__(self):
        self.stats = {}
        self.logger = logging.getLogger(__name__)
```

Next, we want to define a decorator that we can use to mark the coroutines we are interested in:

```
def profile_memory_usage(self, f):
    @wraps(f)
    async def wrapper(*args, **kwargs):
        snapshot = tracemalloc.take_snapshot()
        res = await f(*args, **kwargs)
        self.stats[f.__name__] = tracemalloc.take_snapshot().
        compare_to(snapshot, 'lineno')
        return res

    return wrapper
```

We invoke `tracemalloc.take_snapshot()` to save the current memory allocations before we await the wrapped coroutine.

Then we compute the delta (change) from the first snapshot and save the result for the invoked coroutine:

```
self.stats[f.__name__] = tracemalloc.take_snapshot().compare_
to(snapshot, 'lineno')
```

Note   We lose all but the memory information of the last call to the decorated coroutine function!

We define a convenient `print` method to output the saved `StatisticDiff`:

```
    def print(self):
        for name, stats in self.stats.items():
            for entry in stats:
                self.logger.debug(entry)
```

We create the profiler a (synchronous) context manager to wrap our call to `asyncio.run` while calling `tracemalloc.start` and `tracemalloc.stop`. Furthermore, we print the function-specific memory information upon exiting the context manager scope:

```
def __enter__(self):
    tracemalloc.start()
    return self

def __exit__(self, exc_type, exc_val, exc_tb):
    tracemalloc.stop()
    self.print()
```

After defining the profiler class, we instantiate an instance that we use to decorate a coroutine function and wrap the `asyncio.run` call:

```
profiler = Profiler()

@profiler.profile_memory_usage
async def main():
    pass

with profiler:
    asyncio.run(main())
```

Building a Simple Profiling Library
Problem

In the last recipe, we demonstrated how a profiler class and its method decorator can be used to provide context to the memory allocations of coroutines, but the solution had many drawbacks due to its simplistic nature. These drawbacks include:

- No separation of concerns. The "view" layer (printing out to stdout) and the business logic are stuck together

- Only considers coroutine functions

- Saves only the memory delta of the last coroutine function call

- Hardcodes the type of StatisticDiff generated to lineno

- Does not provide a functionality to profile the execution time of coroutines

Solution

In this example, we refine the profiler class to a small memory and timing profiling library and try to resolve some of the drawbacks we experienced due to the simple nature of the profiling library.

```python
import asyncio
import contextlib
import inspect
import json
import logging
import pickle
import sys
import tracemalloc
from collections import defaultdict, namedtuple
from contextlib import asynccontextmanager
from functools import wraps
from inspect import iscoroutinefunction
from time import time
from tracemalloc import Filter, take_snapshot, start as
tracemalloc_start, \
    stop as tracemalloc_stop
```

```
logging.basicConfig(level=logging.DEBUG, stream=sys.stdout)

Timing = namedtuple("Timing", ["start", "end", "delta"])

class Profiler:

    def __init__(self, key_type="lineno", cumulative=False,
    debug=False, excluded_files=None):
        self.time_stats = defaultdict(list)
        self.memory_stats = defaultdict(dict)
        self.key_type = key_type
        self.cumulative = cumulative
        self.logger = logging.getLogger(__name__)
        self.debug = debug
        if not excluded_files:
            excluded_files = [tracemalloc.__file__,
            inspect.__file__, contextlib.__file__]
        self.excluded_files = excluded_files
        self.profile_memory_cache = False

    def time(self):
        try:
            return asyncio.get_running_loop().time()
        except RuntimeError:
            return time()

    def get_filter(self, include=False):
        return (Filter(include, filter_) for filter_ in
        self.excluded_files)

    def profile_memory(self, f):
        self.profile_memory_cache = True
        if iscoroutinefunction(f):
            @wraps(f)
```

171

```
        async def wrapper(*args, **kwargs):
            snapshot = take_snapshot().filter_traces
            (self.get_filter())
            result = await f(*args, **kwargs)
            current_time = time()
            memory_delta = take_snapshot().filter_traces
            (self.get_filter()).compare_to(snapshot,
            self.key_type, self.cumulative)
            self.memory_stats[f.__name__][current_time] =
            memory_delta
            return result
    else:
        @wraps(f)
        def wrapper(*args, **kwargs):
            snapshot = take_snapshot().filter_trace
            s(self.get_filter())
            result = f(*args, **kwargs)
            current_time = time()
            memory_delta = take_snapshot().filter_traces
            (self.get_filter()).compare_to(snapshot,
            self.key_type, self.cumulative)
            self.memory_stats[f.__name__][current_time] =
            memory_delta
            return result
    return wrapper

def profile_time(self, f):

    if iscoroutinefunction(f):
        @wraps(f)
        async def wrapper(*args, **kwargs):
            start = self.time()
            result = await f(*args, **kwargs)
```

```python
                end = self.time()
                delta = end - start
                self.time_stats[f.__name__].
                append(Timing(start, end, delta))
                return result
        else:
            @wraps(f)
            def wrapper(*args, **kwargs):
                start = self.time()
                result = f(*args, **kwargs)
                end = self.time()
                delta = end - start
                self.time_stats[f.__name__].
                append(Timing(start, end, delta))
                return result
        return wrapper

    def __enter__(self):
        if self.profile_memory_cache:
            self.logger.debug("Starting tracemalloc..")
            tracemalloc_start()

        return self

    def __exit__(self, exc_type, exc_val, exc_tb):
        if self.profile_memory_cache:
            self.logger.debug("Stopping tracemalloc..")
            tracemalloc_stop()
        if self.debug:
            self.print_memory_stats()
            self.print_time_stats()
```

```python
    def print_memory_stats(self):
        for name, stats in self.memory_stats.items():
            for timestamp, entry in list(stats.items()):
                self.logger.debug("Memory measurements for call
                of %s at %s", name, timestamp)

                for stats_diff in entry:
                    self.logger.debug("%s", stats_diff)

    def print_time_stats(self):
        for function_name, timings in self.time_stats.items():
            for timing in timings:
                self.logger.debug("function %s was called at %s
                ms and took: %s ms",
                                        function_name,
                                        timing.start,
                                        timing.delta)

async def read_message(reader, timeout=3):
    data = []
    while True:
        try:
            chunk = await asyncio.wait_for(reader.read(1024),
            timeout=timeout)
            data += [chunk]
        except asyncio.TimeoutError:
            return b"".join(data)

class ProfilerServer:
    def __init__(self, profiler, host, port):
        self.profiler = profiler
        self.host = host
        self.port = port
```

```python
    async def on_connection(self,
                              reader: asyncio.StreamReader,
                              writer: asyncio.StreamWriter):
        message = await read_message(reader)
        logging.debug("Message %s:", message)

        try:
            event = json.loads(message, encoding="UTF-8")
            command = event["command"]
            if command not in ["memory_stats", "time_stats"]:
                raise ValueError(f"{command} is illegal!")

            handler = getattr(self.profiler, command, None)
            if not handler:
                raise ValueError(f"{message} is malformed")
            reply_message = handler

            writer.write(pickle.dumps(reply_message))
            await writer.drain()
        except (UnicodeDecodeError, json.JSONDecodeError,
        TypeError,)as err:
            self.profiler.logger.error("Error occurred while
            transmission: %s", err)
            writer.write(pickle.dumps(err))
            await writer.drain()
        finally:
            writer.close()

class ProfilerClient:
    def __init__(self, host, port):
        self.host = host
        self.port = port
```

```python
    async def send(self, **kwargs):
        message = json.dumps(kwargs)
        reader, writer = await asyncio.open_connection(self.
        host, self.port)
        writer.write(message.encode())
        message = await reader.read()
        writer.close()
        try:
            return pickle.loads(message)
        except pickle.PickleError:
            return None

    async def get_memory_stats(self):
        return await self.send(command="memory_stats")

    async def get_time_stats(self):
        return await self.send(command="time_stats")

@asynccontextmanager
async def start_profiler_server(profiler, host, port):
    profiler_server = ProfilerServer(profiler, host, port)
    try:
        server = await asyncio.start_server(profiler_server.
        on_connection, host, port)
        async with server:
            yield
            await server.serve_forever()
    finally:
        pass

profiler = Profiler(debug=True)

@profiler.profile_time
@profiler.profile_memory
```

```
async def to_be_profiled():
    await asyncio.sleep(3)
    list(i for i in range(10000))

async def main(profiler):
    host, port = "127.0.0.1", 1234
    client = ProfilerClient(host, port)
    async with start_profiler_server(profiler, host, port):
        await to_be_profiled()
        memory_stats = await client.get_memory_stats()
        logging.debug(memory_stats)

try:
    logging.debug("Press CTRL+C to close...")
    with profiler:
        asyncio.run(main(profiler))
except KeyboardInterrupt:
    logging.debug("Closed..")
```

How It Works

The design of this version of the profiling library provides a profiling interface that can be used by coroutine and non-coroutine functions alike. It needs to provide a profiling interface for memory and time complexity. Also, it must expose its current state via a simple TCP endpoint that can be queried via a JSON request and respond with the current state serialized by the pickle module.

Note   If the request fails, there is no retransmission. Furthermore, to avoid blocking the request timeout after three seconds (by default), the timeout parameter can be tweaked.

To save the timing measurements, we generate a lightweight timing entity:

```
Timing = namedtuple("Timing", ["start", "end", "delta"])
```

Next, we create the profiler class that is much like the one from the last example. Except that this time, the whole profiling process is customizable:

```
class Profiler:

    def __init__(self, key_type="lineno", cumulative=False,
    debug=False, excluded_files=None):
        self.time_stats = defaultdict(list)
        self.memory_stats = defaultdict(dict)
        self.key_type = key_type
        self.cumulative = cumulative
        self.logger = logging.getLogger(__name__)
        self.debug = debug
        if not excluded_files:
            excluded_files = [tracemalloc.__file__,
            inspect.__file__, contextlib.__file__]
        self.excluded_files = excluded_files
        self.profile_memory_cache = False
```

The first two parameters—key_type and cumulative—are directly passed to the compare_to method of the tracemalloc.Snapshot instances. The debug flag prints the measurements when exiting the context manager. excluded_files is used to exclude certain files from the memory snapshot via the tracemalloc.Filter API. The profile_memory_cache attribute is used to not invoke tracemalloc.start needlessly, but rather only if at least one memory profile decorator was used. Next, we define two helpers:

```
    def time(self):
        try:
            return asyncio.get_running_loop().time()
```

```
    except RuntimeError:
        return time()

def get_filter(self, include=False):
    return (Filter(include, filter_) for filter_ in self.
    excluded_files)
```

Since our profiler can be used for coroutine functions and non-coroutine functions alike, we need to provide an abstract way to get the current timestamp. Hence, our **time** method. get_filter generates an iterable of tracemalloc.Filter instances to pass to the tracemalloc. Snapshot instances in the memory profiler. The following methods are the heart of the profiler:

```
def profile_memory(self, f):
    self.profile_memory_cache = True
    if iscoroutinefunction(f):
        @wraps(f)
        async def wrapper(*args, **kwargs):
            snapshot = take_snapshot().filter_traces
            (self.get_filter())
            result = await f(*args, **kwargs)
            current_time = time()
            memory_delta = take_snapshot().filter_traces
            (self.get_filter()).compare_to(snapshot,
            self.key_type, self.cumulative)
            self.memory_stats[f.__name__][current_time] =
            memory_delta
            return result
    else:
        @wraps(f)
        def wrapper(*args, **kwargs):
            snapshot = take_snapshot().filter_traces
            (self.get_filter())
```

```
                result = f(*args, **kwargs)
                current_time = time()
                memory_delta = take_snapshot().filter_traces
                (self.get_filter()).compare_to(snapshot,
                self.key_type, self.cumulative)
                self.memory_stats[f.__name__][current_time] =
                memory_delta
                return result
        return wrapper

    def profile_time(self, f):

        if iscoroutinefunction(f):
            @wraps(f)
            async def wrapper(*args, **kwargs):
                start = self.time()
                result = await f(*args, **kwargs)
                end = self.time()
                delta = end - start
                self.time_stats[f.__name__].
                append(Timing(start, end, delta))
                return result
        else:
            @wraps(f)
            def wrapper(*args, **kwargs):
                start = self.time()
                result = f(*args, **kwargs)
                end = self.time()
                delta = end - start
                self.time_stats[f.__name__].
                append(Timing(start, end, delta))
                return result
        return wrapper
```

profile_memory and profile_time are the memory and time profile decorators that we can attach to coroutines and functions alike. They will append the recent memory StatisticDiff for a given (coroutine) function and timestamp (queried by the Profiler.time method) or the execution duration of a call saved as a Timing object per the (coroutine) function.

profile_memory will additionally filter out the excluded_files (as you can see, we use the __file__ attribute of some built-in modules to exclude them by default) from the memory snapshots.

As alluded to, we improve the profiler context manager by invoking tracemalloc.start (tracemalloc_start is an alias) only when necessary and conditionally printing the memory and time stats depending on the debug flag:

```python
def __enter__(self):
    if self.profile_memory_cache:
        self.logger.debug("Starting tracemalloc..")
        tracemalloc_start()

    return self

def __exit__(self, exc_type, exc_val, exc_tb):
    if self.profile_memory_cache:
        self.logger.debug("Stopping tracemalloc..")
        tracemalloc_stop()
    if self.debug:
        self.print_memory_stats()
        self.print_time_stats()
```

The ProfilerServer and ProfilerClient are the foundation of our transportation layer. Both parts use the read_message coroutine function helper to query the reader with a timeout.

```
async def read_message(reader, timeout=3):
    data = []
    while True:
        try:
            chunk = await asyncio.wait_for(reader.read(1024),
            timeout=timeout)
            data += [chunk]
        except asyncio.TimeoutError:
            return b"".join(data)
```

The ProfilerServer responds with a serialized version of the underlying profiler's class ProfilerServer:

```
def __init__(self, profiler, host, port):
    self.profiler = profiler
    self.host = host
    self.port = port
```

The memory_stats and time_stats attributes, if queried with the right attribute names marshaled in a JSON payload, look like this:

```
{
    "command": "memory_stats" | "time_stats"
}
```

The bit that does this handling is the on_connection coroutine method:

```
async def on_connection(self,
                            reader: asyncio.StreamReader,
                            writer: asyncio.StreamWriter):
    message = await read_message(reader)
    logging.debug("Message %s:", message)
```

```
    try:
        event = json.loads(message, encoding="UTF-8")
        command = event["command"]
        if command not in ["memory_stats", "time_stats"]:
            raise ValueError(f"{command} is illegal!")

        handler = getattr(self.profiler, command, None)
        if not handler:
            raise ValueError(f"{message} is malformed")
        reply_message = handler

        writer.write(pickle.dumps(reply_message))
        await writer.drain()
    except (UnicodeDecodeError, json.JSONDecodeError,
    TypeError,)as err:
        self.profiler.logger.error("Error occurred while
        transmission: %s", err)
        writer.write(pickle.dumps(err))
        await writer.drain()
    finally:
        writer.close()
```

The profiler client respects the protocol and returns a valid value if it was able to *unpickle* the message:

```
class ProfilerClient:
    def __init__(self, host, port):
        self.host = host
        self.port = port

    async def send(self, **kwargs):
        message = json.dumps(kwargs)
        reader, writer = await asyncio.open_connection(self.
        host, self.port)
```

```
        writer.write(message.encode())
        message = await reader.read()
        writer.close()
        try:
            return pickle.loads(message)
        except pickle.PickleError:
            return None

    async def get_memory_stats(self):
        return await self.send(command="memory_stats")

    async def get_time_stats(self):
        return await self.send(command="time_stats")
```

We define a start_profiler_server asynccontextmanager that wraps asyncio.start_server and takes care of calling server.serve_ forever(). We need to pass the profiler from the outside, since it decorates functions and methods. Mind you, async with can only be used in the context of a coroutine function body:

```
@asynccontextmanager
async def start_profiler_server(profiler, host, port):
    profiler_server = ProfilerServer(profiler, host, port)
    try:
        server = await asyncio.start_server(profiler_server.
        on_connection, host, port)
        async with server:
            yield
            await server.serve_forever()
    finally:
        pass
```

Next, we decorate our time- and memory-intensive coroutine function `to_be_profiled`:

```
profiler = Profiler(debug=True)

@profiler.profile_time
@profiler.profile_memory
async def to_be_profiled():
    await asyncio.sleep(3)
    list(i for i in range(10000))
```

And query our instance of the `ProfilerServer` with a `ProfilerClient` instance:

```
sync def main(profiler):
    host, port = "127.0.0.1", 1234
    client = ProfilerClient(host, port)
    async with start_profiler_server(profiler, host, port):
        await to_be_profiled()
        memory_stats = await client.get_memory_stats()
        logging.debug(memory_stats)
```

Don't forget to wrap `asyncio.run` with the profiler context manager:

```
try:
    logging.debug("Press CTRL+C to close...")
    with profiler:
        asyncio.run(main(profiler))
except KeyboardInterrupt:
    logging.debug("Closed..")
```

Spotting a Long-Running Coroutine

Problem

You need to spot a coroutine that runs too long.

Solution

We will write a decorator factory that tracks the time a coroutine was running and invokes a formerly passed handler function if it surpasses a certain threshold. Using the sys.set_coroutine_origin_tracking_depth API, we can track the coroutine *origin*, meaning the place where the coroutine was created, with the most recent call first.

```python
import asyncio
import logging
import sys
from functools import wraps

THRESHOLD = 0.5
sys.set_coroutine_origin_tracking_depth(10)

def time_it_factory(handler):
    def time_it(f):
        @wraps(f)
        async def wrapper(*args, **kwargs):
            loop = asyncio.get_running_loop()
            start = loop.time()
            coro = f(*args, **kwargs)
            result = await coro
            delta = loop.time() - start
            handler(coro, delta)
            return result
```

```
        return wrapper

    return time_it
@time_it_factory
def log_time(coro, time_delta):
    if time_delta > THRESHOLD:
        logging.warning("The coroutine %s took more than %s
        ms", coro, time_delta)
        for frame in coro.cr_origin:
            logging.warning("file:%s line:%s function:%s", *frame)
        else:
            logging.warning("Coroutine has no origin !")

@log_time
async def main():
    await asyncio.sleep(1)

asyncio.run(main())
```

How It Works

We define a threshold of 0.5 seconds and make sure that at least 10 frames of a coroutine stack are stored inside the coroutine's cr_origin by invoking sys.set_coroutine_origin_tracking_depth(10):

```
THRESHOLD = 0.5
sys.set_coroutine_origin_tracking_depth(10)
```

Note   The sys.set_coroutine_origin_tracking_depth API replaces the set_coroutine_wrapper() API, which has been deprecated and will be removed in Python version 3.8. See bpo-32591 or the next section for more details.

Next up is our decorator factory:

```
def time_it_factory(handler):
    def time_it(f):
        @wraps(f)
        async def wrapper(*args, **kwargs):
            loop = asyncio.get_running_loop()
            start = loop.time()
            coro = f(*args, **kwargs)
            result = await coro
            delta = loop.time() - start
            handler(coro, delta)
            return result

        return wrapper

    return time_it
```

If you look closely, you might see that the time_it decorator resembles the profiler's profile_time method. It is just more lightweight since it targets only coroutines and calls a handler function with the coro and the time_delta as a parameter:

```
handler(coro,delta)
```

You can decorate a function you intend to use with a coroutine decorator, like so:

```
@time_it_factory
def log_time(coro, time_delta):
    if time_delta > THRESHOLD:
        logging.warning("The coroutine %s took more than %s
        ms", coro, time_delta)
```

```
for frame in coro.cr_origin:
    logging.warning("file:%s line:%s function:%s",
    *frame)
else:
    logging.warning("Coroutine has no origin !")
```

Now the `log_time` decorator will be injected with the currently used coroutine and the time it took to run. As you can see, we use the coroutine `cr_origin` member to print the call chain.

You can then, for instance, use the decorator on the callers of the coroutine if you suspect them to be the source of the bottleneck. Or you can write more sophisticated decorators that do this by automatically using the `decorator_factory`.

Refactoring "Old School" Asyncio Code Problem

You need to find replacements for some of the deprecated APIs and anti-patterns of asyncio.

Solution #1

In this solution, we show examples of deprecated asyncio code alongside the newer code.

```
import asyncio
import sys

async def coro():
    print("This works!")
```

```python
async def ensure_future_deprecated():
    # Up to Python 3.6
    task = asyncio.ensure_future(coro())

    # In Python 3.7+
    task_2 = asyncio.create_task(coro())

async def main():
    pass

# Up to Python 3.6
asyncio.get_event_loop().run_until_complete(main())

# Python 3.7+
asyncio.run(main())

async def wait_deprecated():
    # Passing coroutines objects to wait() directly is deprecated:

    coros = [asyncio.sleep(10), asyncio.sleep(10)]
    done, pending = await asyncio.wait(coros)

    # Use asyncio.create_task

    futures = [asyncio.create_task(coro) for coro in (asyncio.
    sleep(10), asyncio.sleep(10))]
    done, pending = await asyncio.wait(futures)

async def tasks_deprecated(loop):
    # Using Task class methods is deprecated:
    task = asyncio.Task.current_task(loop)
    tasks = asyncio.Task.all_tasks(loop)

    # Use the asyncio module level functions instead:
    task = asyncio.current_task(loop)
    tasks = asyncio.all_tasks(loop)
```

```python
async def coroutine_deprecated():
    @asyncio.coroutine
    def gen_coro():
        yield from asyncio.sleep(1)

    async def native_coroutine():
        await asyncio.sleep(1)

async def passing_loop_deprecated():
    loop = asyncio.get_running_loop()
    # This is deprecated
    await asyncio.sleep(10, loop=loop)
    await asyncio.wait_for(asyncio.create_task(asyncio.
    sleep(10)), 11, loop=loop)
    futures = {asyncio.create_task(asyncio.sleep(10,
    loop=loop))}
    done, pending = await asyncio.wait(futures, loop=loop)

    await asyncio.sleep(10)
    await asyncio.wait_for(asyncio.create_task(asyncio.
    sleep(10)), 11, loop=loop)
    futures = {asyncio.create_task(asyncio.sleep(10))}
    done, pending = await asyncio.wait(futures)

async def coroutine_wrapper_deprecated():
    # set_coroutine_wrapper() and sys.get_coroutine_wrapper()
    will be removed in Python 3.8
    sys.set_coroutine_wrapper(sys.get_coroutine_wrapper())
    # and are deprecated in favor of
    sys.set_coroutine_origin_tracking_depth(sys.get_coroutine_
    origin_tracking_depth())
    # Of course passing sensible values!
```

How It Works

Using asyncio.ensure_future is considered deprecated, but it will not be removed soon to maintain backward compatibility with older versions. asyncio.create_task is to be used now:

```python
async def coro():
    print("This works!")

async def ensure_future_deprecated():
    # Up to Python 3.6
    task = asyncio.ensure_future(coro())

    # In Python 3.7+
    task_2 = asyncio.create_task(coro())
```

To hide complexity away from users who have a simple "one-loop-in-a-process-and-thread" setting, we can use asyncio.run instead of dealing with the somewhat confusing details of asyncio.get_event_loop and the like:

```python
async def main():
    pass

# Up to Python 3.6
asyncio.get_event_loop().run_until_complete(main())

# Python 3.7+
asyncio.run(main())
```

Passing coroutines directly to asyncio.wait is supported but might have a surprising result since this approach schedules the coroutines and wraps them in tasks under the hood. Hence, checking for the coroutines in the returned "done and pending" sets will fail. The recommended way to use asyncio.wait is to schedule the coroutines as task objects first, before passing them:

```
async def wait_deprecated():
    # Passing coroutines objects to wait() directly is deprecated:

    coros = [asyncio.sleep(10), asyncio.sleep(10)]
    done, pending = await asyncio.wait(coros)

    # Use asyncio.create_task

    futures = [asyncio.create_task(coro) for coro in (asyncio.
    sleep(10), asyncio.sleep(10))]
    done, pending = await asyncio.wait(futures)
```

Using asyncio.Task class methods current_task and all_tasks is also considered deprecated. We use asyncio.current_task and asyncio.all_tasks instead:

```
async def tasks_deprecated(loop):
    # Using Task class methods is deprecated:
    task = asyncio.Task.current_task(loop)
    tasks = asyncio.Task.all_tasks(loop)

    # Use the asyncio module level functions instead:
    task = asyncio.current_task(loop)
    tasks = asyncio.all_tasks(loop)
```

Of course, messing around with generator coroutines is considered deprecated and a design mistake. Use native coroutines instead (which disallow yield from in their function bodies):

```
async def coroutine_deprecated():
    @asyncio.coroutine
    def gen_coro():
        yield from asyncio.sleep(1)

    async def native_coroutine():
        await asyncio.sleep(1)
```

Passing a loop parameter was optionally possible in a few APIs, namely:

- `asyncio.sleep`

- `asyncio.wait_for`

- `asyncio.wait`

This has been deprecated as of Python 3.7:

```
async def passing_loop_deprecated():
    loop = asyncio.get_running_loop()
    # This is deprecated
    await asyncio.sleep(10, loop=loop)
    await asyncio.wait_for(asyncio.create_task(asyncio.
    sleep(10)), 11, loop=loop)
    futures = {asyncio.create_task(asyncio.sleep(10,
    loop=loop))}
    done, pending = await asyncio.wait(futures, loop=loop)

    await asyncio.sleep(10)
    await asyncio.wait_for(asyncio.create_task(asyncio.
    sleep(10)), 11, loop=loop)
    futures = {asyncio.create_task(asyncio.sleep(10))}
    done, pending = await asyncio.wait(futures)
```

Also, as mentioned in the last section, using the coroutine wrapper API in the sys module has also been deprecated. It was considered too powerful and generally added too much overhead, in that it was able to change the behavior of *all native coroutines*.

Since the initial idea was to provide a way to track the origin of a coroutine, the sys.*_coroutine_origin_tracking_depth APIs and the cr_origin native coroutine attribute were added:

```python
async def coroutine_wrapper_deprecated():
    # set_coroutine_wrapper() and sys.get_coroutine_wrapper()
    will be removed in Python 3.8
    sys.set_coroutine_wrapper(sys.get_coroutine_wrapper())
    # and are deprecated in favor of
    sys.set_coroutine_origin_tracking_depth(sys.get_coroutine_
    origin_tracking_depth())
    # Of course, passing sensible values!
```

More details can be found in bpo-32591.

Solution #2

Using the ast module, we can find occurrences of generator-based coroutines and other deprecated asyncio APIs. This solution demonstrates how to do so for decorated and non-decorated generator-based coroutines using function bodies. It also detects if you have imported the @asyncio. coroutine decorator using from asyncio import coroutine.

```python
## How to refactor "old school" asyncio code
import argparse
import ast
import asyncio
import functools
import os
from asyncio import coroutine

parser = argparse.ArgumentParser("asyncompat")
parser.add_argument("--path", default=__file__)
```

```
### TEST SECTION ###

@coroutine
def producer():
    return 123

@asyncio.coroutine
def consumer():
    value = yield from producer()
    return value

def consumer2():
    value = yield from producer()
    return value

### TEST SECTION END ###

def is_coroutine_decorator(node):
    return (isinstance(node, ast.Attribute) and
            isinstance(node.value, ast.Name) and
            hasattr(node.value, "id") and
            node.value.id == "asyncio" and node.attr ==
            "coroutine")

def is_coroutine_decorator_from_module(node, *, imported_asyncio):
    return (isinstance(node, ast.Name) and
            node.id == "coroutine" and
            isinstance(node.ctx, ast.Load) and
            imported_asyncio)

class FunctionDefVisitor(ast.NodeVisitor):
    def __init__(self):
        self.source = None
        self.first_run = True
        self.imported_asyncio = False
```

```python
    def initiate_visit(self, source):
        self.source = source.splitlines()
        node = ast.parse(source)
        self.visit(node)
        self.first_run = False
        return self.visit(node)

    def visit_Import(self, node):
        for name in node.names:
            if name.name == "asyncio":
                self.imported_asyncio = True

    def visit_FunctionDef(self, node):
        if self.first_run:
            return

        decorators = list(filter(is_coroutine_decorator,
        node.decorator_list))
        decorators_from_module = list(
            filter(functools.partial(is_coroutine_decorator_from_
            module, imported_asyncio=self.imported_asyncio),
                    node.decorator_list))
        if decorators:
            print(node.lineno, ":", self.source[node.lineno],
            "is an oldschool coroutine!")

        elif decorators_from_module:
            print(node.lineno, ":", self.source[node.lineno],
            "is an oldschool coroutine!")

if __name__ == '__main__':
    v = FunctionDefVisitor()
    args = parser.parse_args()
    path = os.path.isfile(args.path) and os.path.abspath(args.path)
```

```
if not path or not path.endswith(".py"):
    raise ValueError(f"{path} is not a valid path to a
    python file!")
with open(path) as f:
    v.initiate_visit(f.read())
```

How It Works

In this solution, we wanted to demonstrate how to use the `ast` module to find coroutines defined in the old generator decorator fashion. For this matter, we provide two predicate functions that test an `ast` node to see if it contains such a decorator:

```
def is_coroutine_decorator(node):
    return (isinstance(node, ast.Attribute) and
            isinstance(node.value, ast.Name) and
            hasattr(node.value, "id") and
            node.value.id == "asyncio" and node.attr ==
            "coroutine")

def is_coroutine_decorator_from_module(node, *, imported_
asyncio):
    return (isinstance(node, ast.Name) and
            node.id == "coroutine" and
            isinstance(node.ctx, ast.Load) and
            imported_asyncio)
```

Next, we write a two-pass `ast.NodeVisitor` that traverses the program's abstract syntax tree to look for function definitions that contain a `@asyncio.coroutine` or a `@coroutine` decorator, since this is where we could have imported the decorator:

```python
from asyncio import coroutine:

class FunctionDefVisitor(ast.NodeVisitor):
    def __init__(self):
        self.source = None
        self.first_run = True
        self.imported_asyncio = False

    def initiate_visit(self, source):
        self.source = source.splitlines()
        node = ast.parse(source)
        self.visit(node)
        self.first_run = False
        return self.visit(node)

    def visit_Import(self, node):
        for name in node.names:
            if name.name == "asyncio":
                self.imported_asyncio = True
```

In the first pass, we check for the import. We save how asyncio was imported and inject it as an additional parameter into our predicate functions, which we use to filter the function definitions:

```python
def visit_FunctionDef(self, node):
        if self.first_run:
            return

        decorators = list(filter(is_coroutine_decorator,
        node.decorator_list))
        decorators_from_module = list(
            filter(functools.partial(is_coroutine_decorator_
            from_module, imported_asyncio=self.imported_
            asyncio),
                    node.decorator_list))
```

```
    if decorators:
        print(node.lineno, ":", self.source[node.lineno],
        "is an oldschool coroutine!")

    elif decorators_from_module:
        print(node.lineno, ":", self.source[node.lineno],
        "is an oldschool coroutine!")
```

For the sake of our example, we defined a test section as follows:

```
@coroutine
def producer():
    return 123

@asyncio.coroutine
def consumer():
    value = yield from producer()
    return value

def consumer2():
    value = yield from producer()
    return value
```

This should be found by our command-line tool using the
FunctionDefVisitor:

```
if __name__ == '__main__':
    v = FunctionDefVisitor()
    args = parser.parse_args()
    path = os.path.isfile(args.path) and os.path.abspath
    (args.path)
    if not path or not path.endswith(".py"):
        raise ValueError(f"{path} is not a valid path to a
        python file!")
    with open(path) as f:
        v.initiate_visit(f.read())
```

Avoiding Busy Loops

Problem

Busy loops actively poll resources to determine their states. You want to rewrite a (multi-threaded) busy loop doing some I/O more elegantly with asyncio.

Solution

Given the asyncio.Future object, we can await the completion of a coroutine very elegantly.

```python
import asyncio
import random

async def fetch(url, *, fut: asyncio.Future):
    await asyncio.sleep(random.randint(3, 5))  # Simulating work
    fut.set_result(random.getrandbits(1024 * 8))

async def checker(responses, url, *, fut: asyncio.Future):
    result = await fut
    responses[url] = result
    print(result)

async def main():
    loop = asyncio.get_running_loop()
    future = loop.create_future()
    responses = {}
    url = "https://apress.com"
    await asyncio.gather(fetch(url, fut=future),
    checker(responses, url, fut=future))

asyncio.run(main())
```

How It Works

A busy loop is generally considered an anti-pattern, since it is very resource intensive and wasteful of the CPU's time. Given an event loop, we can instead be notified when the resource state has changed. Consider the following example, which uses threads and a busy loop:

```
import random
import threading
import time

def fetch(responses, url, *, lock: threading.Lock):
    time.sleep(random.randint(3, 5))  # Simulating work
    with lock:
        responses[url] = random.getrandbits(1024 * 8)

def checker(responses, url, interval=1, timeout=30, *,
lock: threading.Lock):
    interval, timeout = min(interval, timeout), max(interval,
     timeout)
    while timeout:
        with lock:
            response = responses.get(url)
        if response:
            print(response)
            return
        time.sleep(interval)
        timeout -= interval
    raise TimeoutError()

def main():
    lock = threading.Lock()
    responses = {}
```

```
url = "https://apress.com"
fetcher = threading.Thread(target=fetch, args=(responses,
url,), kwargs=dict(lock=lock))
worker = threading.Thread(target=checker, args=(responses,
url,), kwargs=dict(lock=lock))
for t in (fetcher, worker):
    t.start()

fetcher.join()
worker.join()

if __name__ == '__main__':
    main()
```

The fetch function simulates I/O work by using the time.sleep function. It saves random bytes in a response dict guarded by a threading lock to simulate a returned response:

```
def fetch(responses, url, *, lock: threading.Lock):
    time.sleep(random.randint(3, 5))  # Simulating work
    with lock:
        responses[url] = random.getrandbits(1024 * 8)
```

The checker function, on the other hand, tries to retrieve the response guarded by a lock. If it fails to do so (while responses.get(url) is a false value), it retries until the timeout is reached. If the timeout is reached, it raises a TimeoutError:

```
def checker(responses, url, interval=1, timeout=30, *,
lock: threading.Lock):
    interval, timeout = min(interval, timeout), max(interval,
    timeout)
    while timeout:
        with lock:
            response = responses.get(url)
```

```
    if response:
        print(response)
        return
    time.sleep(interval)
    timeout -= interval
raise TimeoutError()
```

Our main function schedules both functions using threads and the same lock instance. It joins on them to await the busy loop:

```
def main():
    lock = threading.Lock()
    responses = {}

    url = "https://apress.com"
    fetcher = threading.Thread(target=fetch, args=(responses,
    url,), kwargs=dict(lock=lock))
    worker = threading.Thread(target=checker, args=(responses,
    url,), kwargs=dict(lock=lock))
    for t in (fetcher, worker):
        t.start()

    fetcher.join()
    worker.join()
```

asyncio is made for I/O. You can easily create a good example in less space and with explicit preemption of your coroutines simply by using a asyncio.Future object:

```
async def fetch(url, *, fut: asyncio.Future):
    await asyncio.sleep(random.randint(3, 5))   # Simulating work
    fut.set_result(random.getrandbits(1024 * 8))
```

By using an asyncio.Future, we can set the result when it is actually ready and signal to the coroutine that is awaiting the future. This allows it to store the result and handle it (printing it like shown here):

```
async def checker(responses, url, *, fut: asyncio.Future):
    result = await fut
    responses[url] = result
    print(result)
```

In this case, the logical counterpart to threading.Thread.join is asyncio.gather:

```
async def main():
    loop = asyncio.get_running_loop()
    future = loop.create_future()
    responses = {}
    url = "https://apress.com"
    await asyncio.gather(fetch(url, fut=future),
    checker(responses, url, fut=future))

asyncio.run(main())
```

The future instance can be conveniently created by using loop.create_future().

Note   Refrain from instantiating asyncio.Future. You might end up with exotic loop implementations that have enhanced future classes that they only expose through loop.create_future()!

## CHAPTER 9

Working with Network Protocols

Network communication is governed by networking protocols. This is the umbrella term used for rulesets that lay out how data is transported and formatted across (or inside) the boundaries of a network node. For instance, they might define in which byte order a payload is to be transferred, the encoding, the length of the payload, if the payload is retransferred upon a failed attempt, etc.

These networking protocols, if crafted to be fit for one single purpose like transportation or authentication, can interact with each other to a degree where they seem to seamlessly inter-opt.

Well known cases for this pattern are HTTP, FTP, SSH, SFTP, and HTTPS, which leverage more low-level transportation protocols like TCP and UDP, use routing protocols like IP, and use TLS as an authentication or integrity protocol.

These protocols are built around a message-exchange mechanism called the *request-response* model. The party that initiates the communication is usually known as the *client*. The answering party is known as the *server*. Communication that is designed like this involves I/O roundtrip times, where the requester/client/callee awaits a response.

A *synchronous* program that implements such a protocol would wait on any responses that are being pending and hence unnecessarily use CPU time.

© Mohamed Mustapha Tahrioui 2019
M. M. Tahrioui, *asyncio Recipes*, https://doi.org/10.1007/978-1-4842-4401-2_9

Asyncio provides tools to write implementations for these protocols or even craft your own protocol that will run on asyncio's powerful event loop system.

asyncio.BaseProtocol subclasses are asyncio primitives that declare which bytes are transported by the asyncio.BaseTransport subclasses, which on the other hand govern how bytes are sent. asyncio provides four out-of-the-box transportation layers: UDP, TCP, TLS, and subprocess pipes.

The asyncio.BaseProtocol subclasses that are of interest to us are:

- asyncio.Protocol for streaming protocols like TCP and UNIX sockets

- asyncio.BufferedProtocol for implementing streaming protocols with manual control of the receive buffer

- asyncio.DatagramProtocol for implementing datagram (UDP) protocols

- asyncio.SubprocessProtocol for implementing protocols communicating with child processes (unidirectional pipes)

In the highly unlikely case that you want to add more asyncio.BaseTransport subclasses, you need to provide your own loop implementation, since no loop API exposes a way to pass asyncio.BaseTransport factories as an argument through. These can be used to create clients or servers that run on an asyncio.BaseLoop subclass. To create clients/servers for a certain protocol, you pass a protocol factory function to one of the following asyncio.BaseLoop methods:

- loop.create_connection

- loop.create_datagram_endpoint

- loop.create_server

- loop.connect_accepted_socket

- loop.subprocess_shell

- `loop.subprocess_exec`

- `loop.connect_read_pipe`

- `loop.connect_write_pipe`

- `loop.create_unix_connection`

- `loop.create_unix_server`

The different connection methods return different transports. They differ in how they transport the data. There are transports that use sockets of different families like AF_INET, AF_UNIX, etc., and types like SOCK_STREAM (TCP) and SOCK_DGRAM (UDP).

The `asyncio.transports.SubprocessTransport` subclasses communicate via pipes. They are used in the context of subprocesses.

The `create_unix_connection` and `create_unix_server` methods are only available on UNIX hosts. Subprocesses on Windows work only on the `ProactorEventLoop`, as seen in earlier examples:

```
if sys.platform == "win32":
    asyncio.set_event_loop_policy(asyncio.
WindowsProactorEventLoopPolicy())
```

In the course of this chapter, we discuss a subset of the loop methods and some of the `asyncio.BaseProtocol` subclasses that are critical for understanding how these networking primitives are used.

Writing a Protocol Subclass for a Simple Remote Command Server

Problem

We want to implement a server for a custom network protocol with binary payloads in asyncio.

Solution

As established, asyncio provides an implementation of the asyncio. BaseProtocol class that helps us implement network protocols. They define callbacks that are then called by the asyncio.Transport object. They have a strict 1:1 mapping to asyncio.BaseProtocol objects.

Implementing our own simple protocol, we will write a server that receives a serialized Python function and runs it inside of a subprocess pool. It then returns the result to the callee over TCP. For better pickling support, we use the third-party library cloudpickle. It enables us to serialize responses, like functions, that might not be importable.

To install it, we use the following:

```
pipenv install cloudpickle==0.6.1
# or
pip3 install cloudpickle==0.6.1
```

```
import asyncio
import functools
import inspect
import logging
import sys
from multiprocessing import freeze_support, get_context

import cloudpickle as pickle

logging.basicConfig(level=logging.DEBUG, stream=sys.stdout)

def on_error(exc, *, transport, peername):
    try:
        logging.exception("On error: Exception while handling a
        subprocess: %s ", exc)
        transport.write(pickle.dumps(exc))
```

```python
    finally:
        transport.close()
        logging.info("Disconnected %s", peername)

def on_success(result, *, transport, peername, data):
    try:
        logging.debug("On success: Received payload from %s:%s
        and successfully executed:\n%s", *peername, data)
        transport.write(pickle.dumps(result))
    finally:
        transport.close()
        logging.info("Disconnected %s", peername)

def handle(data):
    f, args, kwargs = pickle.loads(data)
    if inspect.iscoroutinefunction(f):
        return asyncio.run(f(*args, *kwargs))

    return f(*args, **kwargs)

class CommandProtocol(asyncio.Protocol):

    def __init__(self, pool, loop, timeout=30):
        self.pool = pool
        self.loop = loop
        self.timeout = timeout
        self.transport = None

    def connection_made(self, transport):
        peername = transport.get_extra_info('peername')
        logging.info('%s connected', peername)
        self.transport = transport
```

```python
    def data_received(self, data):
        peername = self.transport.get_extra_info('peername')
        on_error_ = functools.partial(on_error, transport=self.
        transport, peername=peername)
        on_success_ = functools.partial(on_success,
        transport=self.transport, peername=peername, data=data)
        result = self.pool.apply_async(handle, (data,),
        callback=on_success_, error_callback=on_error_)
        self.loop.call_soon(result.wait)
        self.loop.call_later(self.timeout, self.close, peername)

    def close(self, peername=None):
        try:
            if self.transport.is_closing():
                return
            if not peername:
                peername = self.transport.get_extra_
                info('peername')
        finally:
            self.transport.close()
            logging.info("Disconnecting %s", peername)

async def main():
    loop = asyncio.get_running_loop()
    fork_context = get_context("fork")
    pool = fork_context.Pool()
    server = await loop.create_server(lambda:
    CommandProtocol(pool, loop), '127.0.0.1', 8888)
    try:
        async with server:
            await server.serve_forever()
```

```
    finally:
        pool.close()
        pool.join()

if __name__ == '__main__':
    freeze_support()
    asyncio.run(main())
```

How It Works

We can see in the imports that we will use the multiprocessing.Pool to schedule the serialized function (and its arguments):

```
import asyncio
import inspect
import functools
import logging
import os
import pickle
import sys
from multiprocessing import Pool
```

Since we will use the asynchronous pool.apply_async API for that, we need to provide callbacks that are called on results and errors. We define them outside our asyncio.BaseProtocol class definition:

```
logging.basicConfig(level=logging.DEBUG, stream=sys.stdout)

def on_error(exc, *, transport, peername):
    try:
        logging.exception("On error: Exception while handling a
        subprocess: %s ", exc)
        transport.write(pickle.dumps(exc))
```

```
    finally:
        transport.close()
        logging.info("Disconnected %s", peername)

def on_success(result, *, transport, peername, data):
    try:
        logging.debug("On success: Received payload from %s:%s
        and successfully executed:\n%s", *peername, data)
        transport.write(pickle.dumps(result))
    finally:
        transport.close()
        logging.info("Disconnected %s", peername)

def handle(data):
    f, args, kwargs = pickle.loads(data)
    if inspect.iscoroutinefunction(f):
        return asyncio.run(f(*args,*kwargs))
    return f(*args, **kwargs)
```

The reason we don't have them as methods of the `CommandProtocol`
is that calling `result.wait` on the `ApplyResult` instance will try to pickle
the callbacks provided. Since the callbacks are methods, it will also try to
pickle the instance and fail because of the unpickleable `multiprocessing.`
`Pool` attribute.

An easy solution to this problem is to use functions that are pickleable
(if importable) and then pass additional values via `functools.partial`
(as we will see later). The on-error callback is called when exceptions
are raised inside the process pool. Since we inject the transport instance,
we can transfer the serialized exception back to the callee, who can then
proceed to handle it appropriately.

Of course, we close the transport at the end of the usage to not run
into resource leakages. Very similarly we serialize the result and close the
transport afterward. Using a `try-finally` block, we ensure the transport

is always closed. handle basically deserializes the passed data and tries to unpack it since our "contract" is to send a serialized tuple of a function, a tuple of positional arguments, and a dict with keyword arguments. We don't handle exceptions here since they bubble up and are handled by on_error. The return value is the one passed to on_success.

Next up is the CommandProtocol class. First of all, we define the constructor, which needs to pass us the pool instance to handle the different requests. The loop instance is for scheduling callbacks and the timeout is for force-closing the transport if the result takes too long to compute. A transport attribute is initialized to None to hold a reference to the current transport.

```
Class CommandProtocol(asyncio.BaseProtocol):
    def __init__(self, pool, loop, timeout=30):
        self.pool = pool
        self.loop = loop
        self.timeout = timeout
        self.transport = None
```

Next, we need to implement the callbacks that are invoked by the asyncio.Transport instance:

```
def connection_made(self, transport):
    peername = transport.get_extra_info('peername')
    logging.info('%s connected', peername)
    self.transport = transport
```

command_protocol.connection_made is invoked when a client connects to the server. In that case, we store the IP and port information by querying the transport for the peername. We also store a reference to the transport for further use.

The command_protocol.data_received callback is where the better part of the protocol lies. Here we receive the data, which we then pass to the pool. We do not serialize the data here. Rather we wait for the handle callback to be invoked.

We use functools.partial to pass the transport instance, so that the callbacks can return the payload. We also schedule self.close after self. timeout seconds, which force-closes the transport if it is taking too long.

```
def data_received(self, data):
    peername = self.transport.get_extra_info('peername')

    on_error_ = functools.partial(on_error, transport=self.
    transport, peername=peername)
    on_success_ = functools.partial(on_success,
    transport=self.transport, peername=peername, data=data)

    result = self.pool.apply_async(handle, (data,),
    callback=on_success_, error_callback=on_error_)

    self.loop.call_soon(result.wait)
    self.loop.call_later(self.timeout, self.close, peername)
```

The close method is only invoked when we do not close the transport by querying transport.is_closing(). If it is not closed yet, we close it; otherwise, we try to get the peername and close the transport in a finally block:

```
def close(self, peername=None):
    try:
        if self.transport.is_closing():
            return
        if not peername:
            peername = self.transport.get_extra_
            info('peername')
    finally:
        self.transport.close()
        logging.info("Disconnected %s", peername)
```

To start our server, we need to get a loop instance, get a multiprocessing.Pool instance, and create a CommandProtocol factory that we can pass to loop.create_server.

For that matter, we inline a lambda that returns a new CommandProtocol instance that reuses our pool. Now on every connect, a new CommandProtocol instance is spawned, but we use the same pool instance. We spawn the server on localhost and port 8888. We serve forever and close the pool in the finally block.

```
async def main():
    loop = asyncio.get_running_loop()
    pool = Pool()
    server = await loop.create_server(
        lambda: CommandProtocol(pool, loop),
        '127.0.0.1', 8888)
    try:
        async with server:
            await server.serve_forever()
    finally:
        pool.close()
        pool.join()

asyncio.run(main())
```

Note   The (cloud)pickle package does not protect against malicious code. Don't run this server on networks you do not trust. No measurements were taken to harden this server example to keep it focused on the protocol part.

Writing a Protocol Subclass for a Simple Remote Command Client

Problem

We want to implement a client for a custom network protocol with binary payloads in asyncio.

Solution

Due to limitations of the pickle package, it can only load serialized functions that are importable. Since that is not always the case, this solution is less powerful.

For better pickling support, we will use the third-party library called cloudpickle. It will enable us to serialize locally (client-side) defined and remotely inaccessible functions.

To install it, use the following:

```
pipenv install cloudpickle==0.6.1
# or
pip3 install cloudpickle==0.6.1
```

Given our CommandProtocol we are now equipped to call serialized Python functions.

```
import asyncio
import logging
import cloudpickle as pickle
import sys

logging.basicConfig(level=logging.DEBUG, stream=sys.stdout)
```

```python
class CommandClientProtocol(asyncio.Protocol):
    def __init__(self, connection_lost):
        self._connection_lost = connection_lost
        self.transport = None

    def connection_made(self, transport):
        self.transport = transport

    def data_received(self, data):
        result = pickle.loads(data)
        if isinstance(result, Exception):
            raise result
        logging.info(result)

    def connection_lost(self, exc):
        logging.info('The server closed the connection')
        self._connection_lost.set_result(True)

    def execute_remotely(self, f, *args, **kwargs):
        self.transport.write(pickle.dumps((f, args, kwargs)))

async def remote_function(msg):
    print(msg) # This will be printed out on the host
    return 42

async def main():
    loop = asyncio.get_running_loop()

    connection_lost = loop.create_future()

    transport, protocol = await loop.create_connection(
        lambda: CommandClientProtocol(connection_lost),
        '127.0.0.1', 8888)

    protocol.execute_remotely(remote_function, "This worked!")
```

```
    try:
        await connection_lost
    finally:
        transport.close()

asyncio.run(main())
```

How It Works

First we call the imports and alias the cloudpickle package as pickle:

```
import asyncio
import logging
import cloudpickle as pickle
import sys
```

Next up is our CommandClientProtocol class. We pass an asyncio.
Future instance that we use to make sure our program does not exit
until the connection is lost. Also we initialize an empty attribute for the
asyncio.Transport object:

```
logging.basicConfig(level=logging.DEBUG, stream=sys.stdout)

class CommandClientProtocol(asyncio.Protocol):
    def __init__(self, connection_lost):
        self._connection_lost = connection_lost
        self.transport = None
```

Now the callback functions. They are similar to the CommandProtocol.
When the connection is made, connection_made is called with the
respective transport instance, which we save in the same named attribute:

```
    def connection_made(self, transport):
        self.transport = transport
```

Next, we define the data_received callback, which we also know from the CommandProtocol. The on_error and on_success handler send back either the result of invoking the function or any exceptions that happen in the CommandProtocol.handle method. We deserialize the payload and raise it if it happens to be an exception. Otherwise, we log it.

```python
def data_received(self, data):
    result = pickle.loads(data)
    if isinstance(result, Exception):
        raise result
    logging.info(result)
```

The connection_lost method is invoked if we are not in contact with the server anymore. In that case, we want to signal to our future it is consumed by using future.set_result:

```python
def connection_lost(self, exc):
    logging.info('The server closed the connection')
    self._connection_lost.set_result(True)
```

For convenience, we define the execute_remotely method, which takes a function or coroutinefunction and arguments and then invokes them remotely:

```python
def execute_remotely(self, f, *args, **kwargs):
    self.transport.write(pickle.dumps((f, args, kwargs)))
```

We define a coroutine that is invoked on the server:

```python
async def remote_function(msg):
    print(msg) # This will be printed out on the host
    return 42
```

To connect to the server, we pass a protocol factory to the loop.create_connection method of the currently running loop. Then we invoke our convenience method protocol.execute_remotely.

We await the connection_lost future, which we have passed inside our CommandClientProtocol instance. At last, we close the transport in the finally block.

```
async def main():
    loop = asyncio.get_running_loop()

    connection_lost = loop.create_future()

    transport, protocol = await loop.create_connection(
        lambda: CommandClientProtocol(connection_lost),
        '127.0.0.1', 8888)

    protocol.execute_remotely(remote_function, "This worked!")

    try:
        await connection_lost
    finally:
        transport.close()

asyncio.run(main())
```

Writing a Simple HTTP Server

Problem

You need to build a very simple but functional HTTP server using asyncio.start_server.

Solution

For this matter, we install the third-party httptools package. Follow the installation instructions at https://github.com/MagicStack/httptools. At the point of writing this, you could use:

```
pip3 install httptools==0.0.11
# or
pipenv install httptools==0.0.11
```

Using the httptools module and asyncio.Futures for HTTP parsing, we will write an AsyncioHTTPHandler class, which we will use for an asynchronous HTTP server.

```python
import asyncio
from collections import defaultdict, OrderedDict
from json import dumps
from urllib.parse import urljoin
from wsgiref.handlers import format_date_time

from httptools import HttpRequestParser

class HTTPProtocol():

    def __init__(self, future=None):
        self.parser = HttpRequestParser(self)
        self.headers = {}
        self.body = b""
        self.url = b""
        self.future = future

    def on_url(self, url: bytes):
        self.url = url

    def on_header(self, name: bytes, value: bytes):
        self.headers[name] = value

    def on_body(self, body: bytes):
        self.body = body

    def on_message_complete(self):
        self.future.set_result(self)
```

```python
    def feed_data(self, data):
        self.parser.feed_data(data)

MAX_PAYLOAD_LEN = 65536
DEFAULT_HTTP_VERSION = "HTTP/1.1"
NOT_FOUND = """<!DOCTYPE html>
<html>
  <head>
    <meta charset="UTF-8">
    <title>404 | Page not found</title>
    <meta name="viewport" content="width=device-width, initial-
    scale=1">
    <meta name="description" content="404 Error page">
  </head>
  <body>
    <p>"Sorry ! the page you are looking for can't be found"</p>
  </body>
</html>"""

REASONS = {
    100: "Continue",
    101: "Switching Protocols",
    200: "OK",
    201: "Created",
    202: "Accepted",
    203: "Non-Authoritative Information",
    204: "No Content",
    205: "Reset Content",
    206: "Partial Content",
    300: "Multiple Choices",
    301: "Moved Permanently",
```

```
    302: "Found",
    303: "See Other",
    304: "Not Modified",
    305: "Use Proxy",
    307: "Temporary Redirect",
    400: "Bad Request",
    401: "Unauthorized",
    402: "Payment Required",
    403: "Forbidden",
    404: "Not Found",
    405: "Method Not Allowed",
    406: "Not Acceptable",
    407: "Proxy Authentication Required",
    408: "Request Time-out",
    409: "Conflict",
    410: "Gone",
    411: "Length Required",
    412: "Precondition Failed",
    413: "Request Entity Too Large",
    414: "Request-URI Too Large",
    415: "Unsupported Media Type",
    416: "Requested range not satisfiable",
    417: "Expectation Failed",
    500: "Internal Server Error",
    501: "Not Implemented",
    502: "Bad Gateway",
    503: "Service Unavailable",
    504: "Gateway Time-out",
    505: "HTTP Version not supported"

}
```

```python
class HTTPError(BaseException):
    def __init__(self, status_code):
        assert status_code >= 400
        self.status_code = status_code
        self.reason = REASONS.get(status_code, "")

    def __str__(self):
        return f"{self.status_code} - {self.reason}"

class Response:
    def __init__(self, status_code, headers,
                 http_version=DEFAULT_HTTP_VERSION, body=""):
        self.http_version = http_version
        self.status_code = status_code
        self.headers = headers
        self.reason = REASONS.get(status_code, "")
        self.body = body

    def __str__(self):
        status_line = f"{self.http_version} {self.status_code}
        {self.reason}\r\n"

            headers = "".join(
        (f'"{key}": {value}\r\n' for key, value in self.headers.
        items())
        )
        return f"{status_line}{headers}\r\n{self.body}"

    def get_default_headers():
        return OrderedDict({
          "Date": format_date_time(None).encode("ascii"),
          "Server": AsyncioHTTPHandler.banner
    })
```

```python
def response(headers=None, status_code=200, content_type="text/
html", http_version=DEFAULT_HTTP_VERSION, body=""):
    if not headers:
        headers = get_default_headers()
    headers.update({"Content-Type": content_type,
                    "Content-Length": str(len(body))})
    return Response(status_code, headers, http_version, body)

def json(headers=None, status_code=200, content_type="application/
json", http_version=DEFAULT_HTTP_VERSION, body=None):
    if not body:
        body = {}
    return response(headers, status_code, content_type, http_
version, dumps(body))

class AsyncioHTTPHandler:
    allowed_methods = ["GET"]
    version = 1.0
    banner = f"AsyncioHTTPServer/{version}".encode("ascii")
    default_timeout = 30

    def __init__(self, host, timeout=default_timeout):
        self.host = host
        self.routes = defaultdict(dict)
        self.timeout = timeout

    def route(self, *args, method="GET", path=None):

        def register_me(f):
            nonlocal path, self

            if not path:
                path = f.__name__
            http_method = method.upper()
```

```
                assert http_method in AsyncioHTTPHandler.allowed_
                methods

                if not path.startswith("/"):
                    path = urljoin("/", path)
                self.routes[http_method][path] = f
                return f

        if args:
            f, = args
            return register_me(f)
        return register_me

    async def on_connection(self, reader, writer):
        try:
            request = await asyncio.wait_for(reader.read(MAX_
            PAYLOAD_LEN), self.timeout)
            await self.send(writer, await self.handle(request))
        except HTTPError as err:
            if err.status_code == 404:
                await self.send(writer, response(status_
                code=err.status_code, body=NOT_FOUND))
            elif err.status_code == 405:
                headers = get_default_headers()
                headers.update(Allow=",
                ".join(AsyncioHTTPHandler.allowed_methods))
                await self.send(writer, json(headers, status_
                code=err.status_code))
            else:
                await self.send(writer, json(status_code=err.
                status_code))
        except TimeoutError:
            await self.send(writer, json(status_code=408))
```

```
        finally:
            writer.close()

    async def handle(self, request):
        finish_parsing = asyncio.get_running_loop().create_
        future()
        proto = HTTPProtocol(future=finish_parsing)

         try:
            proto.feed_data(request)
            await finish_parsing
            path = proto.url.decode("UTF-8")
            method = proto.parser.get_method().decode("UTF-8")
        except (UnicodeDecodeError, HttpParserUpgrade):
            raise HTTPError(500)

        if not method.upper() in AsyncioHTTPHandler.allowed_
        methods:
            raise HTTPError(405)

        handler = self.routes[method].get(path)
        if not handler:
            raise HTTPError(404)
        return await handler(self)

    async def send(self, writer, response):
        writer.write(str(response).encode("ascii"))
        await writer.drain()

host = "127.0.0.1"
port = 1234

server = AsyncioHTTPHandler(host)
```

```python
@server.route()
async def test_me(server):
    return json(body=dict(it_works=True))

async def main():
    s = await asyncio.start_server(server.on_connection, host,
    port)
    async with s:
        await s.serve_forever()

try:
    asyncio.run(main())
except KeyboardInterrupt:
    print("Closed..")
```

How It Works

The steps are described in the following sections.

Imports

First the imports:

```python
import asyncio
from collections import defaultdict, OrderedDict
from json import dumps
from urllib.parse import urljoin
from wsgiref.handlers import format_date_time

from httptools import HttpRequestParser
```

Protocol Class Definition

Next, we define an HTTPProtocol class that will interact with the HTTP requests and handle parsing via the httptools.HttpRequestParser. All methods prefixed with on_* will be called upon the respective state given by the suffix of the name. For instance, on_body will be invoked on receiving the body of the HTTP request.

The feed_data method is being passed through to httptools. HttpRequestParser, which enables parsing the HTTP request parsing.

```python
class HTTPProtocol():

    def __init__(self, future=None):
        self.parser = HttpRequestParser(self)

        self.headers = {}
        self.body = b""

        self.url = b""
        self.future = future

    def on_url(self, url: bytes):
        self.url = url

    def on_header(self, name: bytes, value: bytes):
        self.headers[name] = value

    def on_body(self, body: bytes):
        self.body = body

    def on_message_complete(self):
        self.future.set_result(self)

    def feed_data(self, data):
        self.parser.feed_data(data)
```

Global Definitions

Other definitions include the maximal payload size, the default HTTP version of this server, and a small template in the case of a 404 error:

```
MAX_PAYLOAD_LEN = 65536
DEFAULT_HTTP_VERSION = "HTTP/1.1"
NOT_FOUND = """<!DOCTYPE html>
<html>
    <head>
        <meta charset="UTF-8">
        <title>404 | Page not found</title>
        <meta name="viewport" content="width=device-width,
        initial-scale=1">
        <meta name="description" content="404 Error page">
    </head>
    <body>
        <p>"Sorry ! the page you are looking for can't be
        found"</p>
    </body>
</html>"""
```

We also must define some messages that accompany the HTTP status codes:

```
REASONS = {
    100: "Continue",
    # Snip...
    505: "HTTP Version not supported"
}
```

Exception Definition

Next, we define an exception that is raised upon HTTP errors, which refers to status codes greater than or equal to 400:

```
class HTTPError(BaseException):
    def __init__(self, status_code):
        assert status_code >= 400
        self.status_code = status_code
        self.reason = REASONS.get(status_code, "")

    def __str__(self):
        return f"{self.status_code} - {self.reason}"
```

Response Class Definition

For sending out responses to HTTP clients that connect to our HTTP server, we define a convenience class response. An HTTP response contains the status code, headers, the HTTP version, and optionally a body. We override the __str__ method to dump the correct representation of the response for transport (before the encoding).

```
class Response:
    def __init__(self, status_code, headers, http_
    version=DEFAULT_HTTP_VERSION, body=""):
        self.http_version = http_version
        self.status_code = status_code
        self.headers = headers
        self.reason = REASONS.get(status_code, "")
        self.body = body

    def __str__(self):
        status_line = f"{self.http_version} {self.status_code}
        {self.reasone}\r\n"
```

```
        headers = "".join(
            (f'"{key}": {value}\r\n' for key, value in self.
            headers.items())
        )
        return f"{status_line}{headers}\r\n{self.body}"
```

Defining Utilities

Next, we define the default headers as a function that returns an
OrderedDict since the order of the headers is important. Also, the date is
considered to be non-optional in most cases, according to the HTTP/1.1
specification: https://www.w3.org/Protocols/rfc2616/rfc2616-sec14.
html#sec14.18.

```
def get_default_headers():
    return OrderedDict({
        "Date": format_date_time(None).encode("ascii"),
        "Server": AsyncioHTTPHandler.banner
    })
```

The following two functions are used by route handlers to return their
payloads in an appropriate format conveniently. The JSON handler is
based on the response handler, which returns a response object. It adds
a parameter for the Content-Type and calculates the Content-Length
header. Additionally, the JSON handler provides a Content-Type that's
suitable for a JSON payload ("application/json") and returns an empty
JSON body instead of an empty body:

```
def response(headers=None, status_code=200, content_type="text/
html", http_version=DEFAULT_HTTP_VERSION, body=""):
    if not headers:
        headers = get_default_headers()
```

```
headers.update({"Content-Type": content_type,
                "Content-Length": str(len(body))})
return Response(status_code, headers, http_version, body)
```

```
def json(headers=None, status_code=200, content_type="application/
json", http_version=DEFAULT_HTTP_VERSION, body=None):
    if not body:
        body = {}
    return response(headers, status_code, content_type, http_
    version, dumps(body))
```

Defining the AsyncioHTTPHandler

The heart of our HTTP server is the AsyncioHTTPHandler. Its duties are to respond to connection attempts and then try to parse and route the message based on the parsed header information, such as the path, etc.

Additionally, it provides an easy way to register coroutines as handlers to requests. To build the AsyncioHTTPHandler, we define the class attributes allowed_methods, where we store the currently supported HTTP methods. For simplicity, we support the GET method for now. We have a version flag that we can use in our banner, which we encode as ASCII bytes. And we have a default timeout of 30 seconds for HTTP connections.

```
class AsyncioHTTPHandler:
    allowed_methods = ["GET"]
    version = 1.0
    banner = f"AsyncioHTTPServer/{version}".encode("ascii")
    default_timeout = 30
```

Next, we define the __init__ method, where we store the current host and are passed the actual timeout value we want to use. We also initialize a defaultdict with a dict factory as the data structure for our routes.

235

The rationale behind this is that we don't want to defensively access our route table. Rather, we want to receive a false value if there is no handler for a particular route. We store the routes by the HTTP method and the routes.

```
def __init__(self, host, timeout=default_timeout):
    self.host = host
    self.routes = defaultdict(dict)
    self.timeout = timeout
```

The next method is used to register HTTP handlers to the provided path. If not passed, the path defaults to the function name. The method parameter is normalized with `str.upper` and then checked in the `allowed_methods`. If the path does not start with a leading forward slash, it is joined via `urllib.parse.urljoin`. Then the route is saved via the normalized HTTP method and path. The lookup is analogue.

```
def route(self, *args, method="GET", path=None):

    def register_me(f):
        nonlocal path, self

        if not path:
            path = f.__name__
        http_method = method.upper()

        assert http_method in AsyncioHTTPHandler.allowed_methods

        if not path.startswith("/"):
            path = urljoin("/", path)
        self.routes[http_method][path] = f
        return f
```

```
if args:
    f, =args
    return register_me(f)
return register_me
```

This last part of the decorator ensures that you can use it either as @server.route or @server.route():

```
if args:
    f, =args
    return register_me(f)
return register_me
```

The on_connection coroutine method is the entry point to the HTTP server. It handles all the incoming HTTP requests. First the request is awaited for the timeout period via asyncio.wait_for and reader.read.

If it times out, we send an HTTP response with HTTP status 408 - request timeout. If we receive a payload as big as MAX_PAYLOAD_LEN or smaller, we pass the payload to self.handle for parsing and either receive a response object back or raise an HTTPError. If the error stems from a miss in the route lookup, we send an HTTP response with a 404-status code.

If a client requests a method that is not allowed, we send an HTTP response with a 405-status code. The HTTP specification requires us to send an Allow header with a comma-separated list of all the allowed HTTP methods.

```
async def on_connection(self, reader, writer):
    try:
        request = await asyncio.wait_for(reader.read(MAX_
        PAYLOAD_LEN), self.timeout)
        await self.send(writer, await self.handle(request))
    except HTTPError as err:
```

```
        if err.status_code == 404:
            await self.send(writer, response(status_
            code=err.status_code, body=NOT_FOUND))
        elif err.status_code==405:
            headers = get_default_headers()
            headers.update(Allow=",
            ".join(AsyncioHTTPHandler.allowed_methods))
            await self.send(writer, json(headers,status_
            code=err.status_code))
        else:
            await self.send(writer, json(status_code=err.
            status_code))
    except TimeoutError:
        await self.send(writer, json(status_code=408))
    finally:
        writer.close()
```

In self.handle, we instantiate a new HttpProtocol instance to handle the response. As of this writing, we can handle the following issues:

- An HTTP header that's not UTF-8 decodable or an HTTP Upgrade request raises an HTTPError with 500, which is the "Internal Error" HTTP status code.

- A non-allowed HTTP method raises an HTTPError with 405, which is the "Not allowed" HTTP status code.

- A failed route lookup raises an HTTPError with 404, which is the (infamous) "Not found" HTTP status code.

We pass a future object into the HTTPProtocol instance, which is set when the whole request is handled. After being awaited, the HTTPProtocol instance contains the request past and method.

```python
async def handle(self, request):
    finish_parsing = asyncio.get_running_loop().create_
    future()
    proto = HTTPProtocol(future=finish_parsing)

    try:
        proto.feed_data(request)
        await finish_parsing
        path = proto.url.decode("UTF-8")
        method = proto.parser.get_method().decode("UTF-8")
    except (UnicodeDecodeError, HttpParserUpgrade):
        raise HTTPError(500)

    if not method.upper() in AsyncioHTTPHandler.allowed_
    methods:
        raise HTTPError(405)

    handler = self.routes[method].get(path)
    if not handler:
        raise HTTPError(404)
    return await handler(self)
```

Finally, we define a convenience method for writing to the
StreamWriter in an ASCII encoding (we do not support charsets yet) and
use drain afterward to make sure the payload is transported.

```python
async def send(self, writer, response):
    writer.write(str(response).encode("ascii"))
    await writer.drain()
```

Starting the Web Server

To start the web server and expose a coroutine method, we create
AsyncioHTTPHandler under the loopback IP address and port 1234. We
then write a handler for the /test_me route and register it via @server.
route. By default, it will be available under /<function_name>, as
explained in the decorator section.

```
host = "127.0.0.1"
port = 1234

server = AsyncioHTTPHandler(host)

@server.route
async def test_me(server):
    return json(body=dict(it_works=True))
```

The important bit here is the call to asyncio.start_server, which
returns a TCP server instance that uses our callback on every new
connection under the given host and port:

```
async def main():
    s = await asyncio.start_server(server.on_connection, host, port)
    async with s:
        await s.serve_forever()

try:
    asyncio.run(main())
except KeyboardInterrupt:
    print("Closed..")
```

We can test it via Python like this:

```
import urllib.request
with urllib.request.urlopen("http://127.0.0.1:1234/test_me") as f:
    print(f.read().decode())
```

Or we could use `curl`:

```
→ curl http://127.0.0.1:1234/test_me
{"it_works": true}%
```

Executing Shell Commands Remotely Over SSH

Problem

You want to write a small library that can execute remote commands defined in Python and resembling OS commands.

Solution

SSH is a network protocol for secure remote login and securely accessing remote services. It establishes a secure channel between a client and a server in an untrusted network. To do this, it usually runs on top of TCP/IP and provides features like integrity protection, encryption, and strong server authentication.

The OpenSSH suite offers an SSH client implementation. The installation of the OpenSSH suite is outlined in the bottom.

The example leverages the OpenSSH userland tools by writing subprocess wrappers around them. To provide a cross-platform experience, we deploy a decorator pattern where we can pass different system commands per OS using keyword parameters.

```
import asyncio
import getpass
import inspect
import logging
import shutil
```

```python
import subprocess
import sys
import itertools
from functools import wraps

logging.basicConfig(level=logging.INFO)

class NotFoundError(BaseException):
    pass

class ProcessError(BaseException):
    def __init__(self, return_code, stderr):
        self.return_code = return_code
        self.stderr = stderr

    def __str__(self):
        return f"Process returned non 0 return code {self.
        return_code}.\n" \
                f"{self.stderr.decode('utf-8')}"

def get_ssh_client_path():
    executable = shutil.which("ssh")
    if not executable:
        raise NotFoundError(
            "Could not find ssh client. You can install OpenSSH
            from https://www.OpenSSH.com/portable.html.\nOn Mac
            OSX we recommend using brew: brew install OpenSSH.\
            nOn Linux systems you should use the package
            manager of your choice, like so. apt-get install
            OpenSSH\nOn windows you can use Chocolatey: choco
            install OpenSSH.")
    return executable
```

```python
def get_ssh_client_path():
    executable = shutil.which("ssh")
    if not executable:
        raise NotFoundError(
            "Could not find ssh client. You can install OpenSSH
            from https://www.OpenSSH.com/portable.html.\nOn Mac
            OSX we recommend using brew: brew install OpenSSH.
            \nOn Linux systems you should use the package
            manager of your choice, like so: apt-get install
            OpenSSH\nOn windows you can use Chocolatey: choco
            install OpenSSH.")
    return executable

class Connection:
    def __init__(self, user=None, host="127.0.0.1", port=22,
    timeout=None, ssh_client=None):
        self.host = host
        self.port = port
        if not user:
            user = getpass.getuser()
        self.user = user
        self.timeout = timeout
        if not ssh_client:
            ssh_client = get_ssh_client_path()
        self.ssh_client = ssh_client

    async def run(self, *cmds, interactive=False):
        commands = [self.ssh_client,
                    f"{self.user}@{self.host}",
                    f"-p {self.port}",
                    *cmds]
        logging.info(" ".join(commands))
```

```python
        proc = await asyncio.create_subprocess_exec(*commands,
                                                    stdin=subprocess.
                                                    PIPE, stdout=
                                                    subprocess.
                                                    PIPE, stderr=
                                                    subprocess.
                                                    PIPE, )
    if not interactive:
        stdout, stderr = await asyncio.wait_for(proc.
        communicate(), self.timeout)

        if proc.returncode != 0:
            raise ProcessError(proc.returncode, stderr)

        return proc, stdout, stderr
    else:
        return proc, proc.stdout, proc.stderr

def command(*args, interactive=False, **kwargs):
    def outer(f):
        cmd = f.__name__
        for key, value in kwargs.items():
            if sys.platform.startswith(key) and value:
                cmd = value

        if inspect.isasyncgenfunction(f):
            @wraps(f)
            async def wrapper(connection, *args):
                proc, stdout, stderr = await connection.
                run(shutil.which(cmd), *args,
                interactive=interactive)

                async for value in f(proc, stdout, stderr):
                    yield value
```

```
        else:
            @wraps(f)
            async def wrapper(connection, *args):
                proc, stdout, stderr = await connection.
                run(shutil.which(cmd), *args,
                interactive=interactive)
                return await f(proc, stdout, stderr)

        return wrapper

    if not args:
        return outer
    else:
        return outer(*args)

@command(win32="dir")
async def ls(proc, stdout, stderr):
    for line in stdout.decode("utf-8").splitlines():
        yield line

@command(win32="tasklist", interactive=True)
async def top(proc, stdout, stderr):
    c = itertools.count()

    async for value in stdout:
        if next(c) >1000:
            break
        print(value)

async def main():
    con = Connection()
    try:
        async for line in ls(con):
            print(line)
```

```
        await top(con)

    except Exception as err:
        logging.error(err)

if sys.platform == "win32":
    asyncio.set_event_loop_policy(asyncio.
    WindowsProactorEventLoopPolicy())

asyncio.run(main())
```

How It Works

Assumptions

Note that this code makes assumptions about the OpenSSH client on your machine. It assumes that you have an OpenSSH daemon running on your machine and the OpenSSH server authenticates via a certificate that you have configured in the SSH configuration. It disregards that the first new connection attempt might require a validity confirmation of the offered fingerprint.

First, we need to install an OpenSSH client (if not already installed on your system). You can install OpenSSH from `https://www.OpenSSH.com/portable.html`.

- On MacOS X, we recommend using brew: `brew install OpenSSH`

- On Linux systems, you should use the package manager of your choice, like so: `apt-get install OpenSSH`

- On Windows, you can use Chocolatey: `choco install OpenSSH`

Imports

We will start by importing the required modules:

```
import asyncio
import inspect
import logging
import shutil
import subprocess
import sys
import itertools
from functools import wraps
import getpass

logging.basicConfig(level=logging.INFO)
```

Defining Exceptions

Next we define some exception classes that might occur inside our program:

```
class NotFoundError(BaseException):
    pass
```

This exception is raised if the user did not install the OpenSSH client on his system.

```
class ProcessError(BaseException):
    def __init__(self, return_code, stderr):
        self.return_code = return_code
        self.stderr = stderr

    def __str__(self):
        return f"Process returned non 0 return code {self.
        return_code}.\n" \
                f"{self.stderr.decode('utf-8')}"
```

This exception is raised on a non-zero return code, which indicates an error code. Next, we write a little helper to get the path to the open SSH client. It raises our defined NotFoundError if it cannot retrieve the path to the OpenSSH client.

```
def get_ssh_client_path():
    executable = shutil.which("ssh")
    if not executable:
        raise NotFoundError("Could not find ssh client. You can
        install OpenSSH from https://www.OpenSSH.com/portable.
        html.\nOn Mac OSX we recommend using brew: brew install
        OpenSSH.\nOn Linux systems you should use the package
        manager of your choice, like so: apt-get install
        OpenSSH\nOn windows you can use Chocolatey: choco
        install OpenSSH.")
    return executable
```

Defining a Connection Class

A connection class encapsulates a simple subset of the information we need in order to have a working minimal wrapper around the OpenSSH client. The connection class captures:

- User

- Host

- Port

- Timeout

- Path to the OpenSSH client

```
class Connection:
    def __init__(self, user=None, host="127.0.0.1", port=22,
    timeout=None, ssh_client=None):
        self.host = host
        self.port = port
        if not user:
            user = getpass.getuser()
        self.user = user
        self.timeout = timeout
        if not ssh_client:
            ssh_client = get_ssh_client_path()
        self.ssh_client = ssh_client
```

The connection class receives a method that runs the commands that are passed to it with the given user, host, port, timeout, and interpreter.

Note   If you run interactive programs like `top`, you might run into issues because awaiting the `Process.communicate()` coroutine will block until it raises the timeout. The purpose of the interactive flag is to return the `stdout` and `stderr` pipes instead of awaiting `Process.communicate()` to read from them for us.

In this case, the return code of the program is not clear, so we do not check it!

```
    async def run(self, *cmds, interactive=False):
        commands = [self.ssh_client,
                    f"{self.user}@{self.host}",
                    f"-p {self.port}",
                    *cmds]
        logging.info(" ".join(commands))
```

```
    proc = await asyncio.create_subprocess_exec(*commands,
                                        stdin=subprocess.
                                        PIPE, stdout=
                                        subprocess.PIPE,
                                        stderr=subprocess.
                                        PIPE, )
if not interactive:
    stdout, stderr = await asyncio.wait_for(proc.
    communicate(), self.timeout)

    if proc.returncode != 0:
        raise ProcessError(proc.returncode, stderr)

    return proc, stdout, stderr
else:
    return proc, proc.stdout, proc.stderr
```

Defining a Command Decorator

The command wrapper does the heavy lifting in terms of OS operability and finding the correct path to our executable.

We can pass the sys.platform names win32, darwin, linux, or cygwin as keyword argument keys to provide a command alias for the target platforms.

The command name defaults to the function name. The interactive flag is passed to connection.run and its purpose and semantics are defined above.

We need to differentiate between async generators and coroutines for our wrapper, because we might want to use the yield keyword inside our command functions.

The commands are expected to have a signature that receives a process instance and a stdout/stderr buffer (bytes), or an async generator that can be queried for the lines depending on the interactive flag, in that particular order:

```
def command(*args, interactive=False, **kwargs):
    def outer(f):
        cmd = f.__name__
        for key, value in kwargs.items():
            if sys.platform.startswith(key) and value:
                cmd = value

        if inspect.isasyncgenfunction(f):
            @wraps(f)
            async def wrapper(connection, *args):
                proc, stdout, stderr = await connection.
                run(shutil.which(cmd), *args,
                interactive=interactive)

                async for value in f(proc, stdout, stderr):
                    yield value
        else:
            @wraps(f)
            async def wrapper(connection, *args):
                proc, stdout, stderr = await connection.
                run(shutil.which(cmd), *args,
                interactive=interactive)
                return await f(proc, stdout, stderr)

        return wrapper
```

This part is so we can use @command or @command() in case we are satisfied with the default options.

```
if not args:
    return outer
else:
    return outer(*args)
```

Remote Command Examples

We define two examples of remote commands. One is the ls command. Its Windows equivalent is dir, so we pass it with a win32 key to the command decorator.

```
@command(win32="dir")
async def ls(proc, stdout, stderr):
    for line in stdout.decode("utf-8").splitlines():
        yield line
```

We also sport an example for an interactive program top.

Note   There is no non-GUI equivalent to top on Windows (to our knowledge), so we used tasklist, which resembles ps.

Since calling process.communicate would block, we instead asynchronously iterate on the stdout stream for 1,000 lines:

```
@command(win32="tasklist", interactive=True)
async def top(proc, stdout, stderr):
    c = itertools.count()
    async for value in stdout:
        if next(c) >1000:
            break
        print(value)
```

Invoking the Commands

This is how we invoke the commands. We pass the connection instance to them and await them if they are coroutines or consume them via `async` for if they are async generators:

```
async def main():
    con = Connection()
    try:
        async for line in ls(con):
            print(line)

        await top(con)

    except Exception as err:
        logging.error(err)
```

This part is necessary since the `SelectorEventLoop`, which is the asyncio default, does not provide subprocess support on Windows:

```
if sys.platform == "win32":
    asyncio.set_event_loop_policy(asyncio.
    WindowsProactorEventLoopPolicy())

asyncio.run(main())
```

## CHAPTER 10

Preventing Common Asyncio Mistakes

Asyncio comes with mistakes of its own. For example, you can forget to await a coroutine, write code that is blocking for too long, or run into data races and deadlocks. Errors can occur inside scheduled tasks, coroutines, and event loops. All of this-in addition to the complexity of learning new APIs and concepts like coroutines and event loops-can discourage people from using asyncio. In this chapter, we learn about common places where mistakes are made and how to pinpoint them, the standard asyncio ways of handling exceptions, and how to craft our own solutions when no corresponding asyncio API is available.

Handling Asyncio-Related Exceptions

Problem

In this example, we find out where we can-but not necessarily should-intercept exceptions that we raise in different asyncio-related scenarios.

Solution #1

As usual, exceptions can bubble up from business code and third-party libraries up to the callee. The exceptions are raised along the chain of

M. M. Tahrioui, *asyncio Recipes*, https://doi.org/10.1007/978-1-4842-4401-2_10

callers up to the outermost frame. Since asyncio introduces new ways to schedule functions and coroutine calls, it is not straightforward anymore where to handle respective exceptions. In this solution, we shed light on how to handle exceptions inside coroutines.

```python
import asyncio
import sys

class MockException(Exception):
    def __init__(self, message):
        self.message = message

    def __str__(self):
        return self.message

async def raiser(text):
    raise MockException(text)

async def main():
    raise MockException("Caught mock exception outside the
    loop. The loop is not running anymore.")

try:
    asyncio.run(main())
except MockException as err:
    print(err, file=sys.stderr)

async def main():
    await raiser("Caught inline mock exception outside the loop."
                "The loop is not running anymore.")

try:
    asyncio.run(main(), debug=True)
except MockException as err:
    print(err, file=sys.stderr)
```

```
async def main():
    try:
        await raiser("Caught mock exception raised in an
                    awaited coroutine outside the loop."
                    "The loop is still running.")
    except MockException as err:
        print(err, file=sys.stderr)

asyncio.run(main(), debug=True)
```

How It Works

We have divided Solution #1 and Solution #2 in the exception handling for exceptions raised inside the loop.call_* methods and the ones raised by coroutines.

The solution for coroutines is simple. You need to guard the awaits with a try-except block if you want to handle exceptions. If not handled, the exception will bubble up to the code that started your loop (asyncio. run or more low-level mechanisms). The first part defines a convenience Exception class that makes printing the error easier:

```
import asyncio
import sys

class MockException(Exception):
    def __init__(self, message):
        self.message = message

    def __str__(self):
        return self.message
```

We also define a coroutine that raises a MockException when we chain awaits and have exceptions in between:

```
async def raiser(text):
    raise MockException(text)
```

Next, we run our main method and show some inline exception raising:

```
async def main():
    raise MockException("Caught mock exception outside the
    loop. The loop is not running anymore.")
```

We decide to catch the exception from the outside, which has the drawback that the loop is not running anymore:

```
try:
    asyncio.run(main())
except MockException as err:
    print(err, file=sys.stderr)
```

It is trivially possible to catch it inline, so we skip demonstrating that case and show the more interesting case of chained coroutines with an inline try-except block:

```
async def main():
    try:
        await raiser("Caught mock exception raised in an
                      awaited coroutine outside the loop."
                    "The loop is still running.")
    except MockException as err:
        print(err, file=sys.stderr)

asyncio.run(main(), debug=True)
```

Here, we catch the exception that is raised by the raiser coroutine inside the parent coroutine.

> **Note**   The loop is still running in this case after the exception
> handling. We caught the exception at the point where the coroutine
> was awaited, which is the crucial part.

Solution #2

In this solution, we discuss how to handle exceptions raised inside the
`loop.call_*` callback scheduling methods.

```python
import asyncio
import sys

class MockException(Exception):
    def __init__(self, message):
        self.message = message

    def __str__(self):
        return self.message

def raiser_sync(text):
    raise MockException(text)

async def main():
    loop = asyncio.get_running_loop()
    loop.call_soon(raiser_sync, "You cannot catch me like this!")
    await asyncio.sleep(3)

try:
    asyncio.run(main(), debug=True)
except MockException as err:
    print(err, file=sys.stderr)
```

```python
async def main():
    try:
        loop = asyncio.get_running_loop()
        loop.call_soon(raiser_sync, "You cannot catch me like
        this!")
    except MockException as err:
        print(err, file=sys.stderr)
    finally:
        await asyncio.sleep(3)

asyncio.run(main(), debug=True)

def exception_handler(loop, context):
    exception = context.get("exception")
    if isinstance(exception, MockException):
        print(exception, file=sys.stderr)
    else:
        loop.default_exception_handler(context)
async def main():
    loop: asyncio.AbstractEventLoop = asyncio.get_running_loop()
    loop.set_exception_handler(exception_handler)
    loop.call_soon(raiser_sync, "Finally caught the loop.call_*
    mock exception!")

asyncio.run(main(), debug=True)
```

How It Works

In this example, we demonstrate how to catch the errors raised by the
loop.call_* methods. Similar to Solution #1, we define our boilerplates:

```python
import asyncio
import sys
```

```
class MockException(Exception):
    def __init__(self, message):
        self.message = message

    def __str__(self):
        return self.message

def raiser_sync(text):
    raise MockException(text)
```

Next, we try to catch the exceptions raised by loop.call_soon at different points (outside the asyncio.run call and at the loop.call_soon call) to no avail:

```
async def main():
    loop = asyncio.get_running_loop()
    loop.call_soon(raiser_sync, "You cannot catch me like this!")
    await asyncio.sleep(3)

try:
    asyncio.run(main(), debug=True)
except MockException as err:
    print(err, file=sys.stderr)

async def main():
    try:
        loop = asyncio.get_running_loop()
        loop.call_soon(raiser_sync, "You cannot catch me like
        this!")
    except MockException as err:
        print(err, file=sys.stderr)
    finally:
        await asyncio.sleep(3)

asyncio.run(main(), debug=True)
```

The right way to catch a `loop.call_*` call is via the `loop.set_exception_handler` API. We need to define an exception handler that will get the currently running loop and a `dict` object containing the following key-value pairs:

- `message`: Error message
- `exception` (optional): Exception object
- `future` (optional): `asyncio.Future` instance
- `handle` (optional): `asyncio.Handle` instance
- `protocol` (optional): Protocol instance
- `transport` (optional): Transport instance
- `socket` (optional): `socket.socket` instance

Our simple exception handler handles all the `MockExceptions` that we define and relays to the `loop.default_exception_handler` in the other cases.

We could also re-raise the exception if we think we have handled all the non-fatal exception cases, but this is up to the developer to decide.

```python
def exception_handler(loop, context):
    exception = context.get("exception")
    if isinstance(exception, MockException):
        print(exception, file=sys.stderr)
    else:
        loop.default_exception_handler(context)

async def main():
    loop: asyncio.AbstractEventLoop = asyncio.get_running_loop()
    loop.set_exception_handler(exception_handler)
    loop.call_soon(raiser_sync, "Finally caught the loop.call_* mock exception!")

asyncio.run(main(), debug=True)
```

Spotting a Long-Running Task

Problem

Coroutines are the first level citizens of asyncio. They operate inside the event loop using Task objects. What if we wanted to know in detail how long our task runs?

Solution

We will write a Task wrapper that records how long our tasks run and teach our loop to create instances of that type.

```
import asyncio
import logging

logging.basicConfig(level=logging.DEBUG)

class MonitorTask(asyncio.Task):

    def __init__(self, coro, *, loop):
        super().__init__(coro, loop=loop)
        self.start = loop.time()
        self.loop = loop

    def __del__(self):
        super(MonitorTask, self).__del__()
        self.loop = None

    def __await__(self):
        it = super(MonitorTask, self).__await__()

        def awaited(self):
            try:
                for i in it:
                    yield i
```

```python
                except BaseException as err:
                    raise err
            finally:
                try:
                    logging.debug("%r took %s ms to run", self,
                    self.loop.time() - self.start)
                except:
                    logging.debug("Could not estimate endtime
                    of %r")

        return awaited(self)

    @staticmethod
    def task_factory(loop, coro):
        task = MonitorTask(coro, loop=loop)
        # The traceback is truncated to hide internal calls in
        # asyncio show only the traceback from user code
        if task._source_traceback:
            del task._source_traceback[-1]
        return task

async def work():
    await asyncio.sleep(1)

async def main():
    loop = asyncio.get_running_loop()
    loop.set_task_factory(MonitorTask.task_factory)
    await asyncio.create_task(work())

asyncio.run(main(), debug=True)
```

How It Works

First, we write our subclass `MonitorTask` in which we store a reference to our current loop. To avoid a reference circle, we set it to None in __del__:

```
class MonitorTask(asyncio.Task):
    def __init__(self, coro, *, loop):
        super().__init__(coro, loop=loop)
        self.start = loop.time()
        self.loop = loop

    def __del__(self):
        super(MonitorTask, self).__del__()
        self.loop = None
```

Next, we override the __await__ function to be able to call our timing logic *after* the task is completely consumed. For this matter, we await the awaitable returned by the super call and re-raise all exceptions that may occur. Using a `finally` block, we reliably time when the task was awaited:

```
    def __await__(self):
        it = super(MonitorTask, self).__await__()

        def awaited(self):
            try:
                for i in it:
                    yield i
            except BaseException as err:
                raise err
            finally:
                try:
                    logging.debug("%r took %s ms to run", self,
                    self.loop.time() - self.start)
```

```
        except:
            logging.debug("Could not estimate endtime
            of %r")

    return awaited(self)
```

Note   The for i in it: yield i syntax is equivalent to a
yield from statement but, unlike yield from, it can be used
syntactically in a function that's not decorated by asyncio.
coroutine.

The most important part is arguably the task factory. It creates
MonitorTask objects and truncate the traceback so the outputs show only
user code information:

```
@staticmethod
def task_factory(loop, coro):
    task = MonitorTask(coro, loop=loop)
    # The traceback is truncated to hide internal calls in
    # asyncio show only the traceback from user code
    if task._source_traceback:
        del task._source_traceback[-1]
    return task
```

Next, we set our task factory on the loop via loop.set_task_factory
and create a task using asyncio.create_task.

The duration of our call to work() will be logged via the logging module.

```
async def work():
    await asyncio.sleep(1)
```

```
async def main():
    loop = asyncio.get_running_loop()
    loop.set_task_factory(MonitorTask.task_factory)
    await asyncio.create_task(work())

asyncio.run(main(), debug=True)
```

For more sophisticated instrumentation, we could use the asyncio.
Task methods asyncio.Task.print_stack or asyncio.Task.get_stack.

Spotting a Long-Running Callback
Problem

Writing a custom task class for a day-to-day use case like spotting long-running callbacks is too complicated.

Solution

We can use a much simpler API to spot a long-running callback (scheduled via loop.call_*). asyncio natively provides the slow_callback_duration property in its loops to achieve the same effect as in the last example.

```
import asyncio
import time

def slow():
    time.sleep(1.5)

async def main():
    loop = asyncio.get_running_loop()
    # This will print a debug message if the call takes more
    than 1 second
```

```
    loop.slow_callback_duration = 1
    loop.call_soon(slow)

asyncio.run(main(), debug=True)
```

How It Works

Using the `loop.slow_callback_duration` attribute, we control at which threshold in seconds the loop prints the traceback for a long-running callback. This example will notify us that our `slow()` callback exceeded the threshold and print out the information on `stderr`.

Building a Coroutine Debugging Macro Library

Problem

Using our knowledge about how errors are handled in asyncio, we want to write a little library that helps us find exceptions when they occur in our coroutines.

Solution

For this solution, we use the `pdb` module in three instances:

- Inject `pdb.post_mortem` in an `except` clause around all non-caught exceptions

- Inject `pdb.set_trace` before the call

- Inject `pdb.set_trace` after the call

Our design goals for our debugging macro library are as follows:

- Not to be invasive on our code, meaning write as little code for debugging as possible

- (Virtually) no execution speed penalty if we do not have the debugging mechanisms enabled to avoid timing-related bugs to be obfuscated

```python
import argparse
import inspect
import os
import pdb
from functools import wraps
import asyncio

def get_asyncio_debug_mode_parser():
    parser = argparse.ArgumentParser()
    parser.add_argument("--asyncio-debug", action="store_true",
    dest="__asyncio_debug__", default=False)
    return parser

def is_asyncio_debug_mode(parser=get_asyncio_debug_mode_parser()):
    return parser and parser.parse_args().__asyncio_debug__ or
    os.environ.get("CUSTOM_ASYNCIO_DEBUG")

__asyncio_debug__ = is_asyncio_debug_mode()

def post_mortem(f):
    if not __asyncio_debug__:
        return f

    if inspect.isasyncgenfunction(f):
        @wraps(f)
        async def wrapper(*args, **kwargs):
```

```python
        try:
            async for payload in f(*args, **kwargs):
                yield payload
        except BaseException as err:
            pdb.post_mortem()
            raise err

    else:
        @wraps(f)
        async def wrapper(*args, **kwargs):
            try:
                return await f(*args, **kwargs)
            except BaseException as err:
                pdb.post_mortem()
                raise err

    return wrapper

def pre_run(f):
    if not __asyncio_debug__:
        return f

    if inspect.isasyncgenfunction(f):
        @wraps(f)
        async def wrapper(*args, **kwargs):
            pdb.set_trace()
            async for payload in f(*args, **kwargs):
                yield payload

    else:
        @wraps(f)
        async def wrapper(*args, **kwargs):
            pdb.set_trace()
            return await f(*args, **kwargs)
```

```
        return wrapper

def post_run(f):
    if not __asyncio_debug__:
        return f

    if inspect.isasyncgenfunction(f):
        @wraps(f)
        async def wrapper(*args, **kwargs):
            async for payload in f(*args, **kwargs):
                yield payload
            pdb.set_trace()

    else:
        @wraps(f)
        async def wrapper(*args, **kwargs):
            result = await f(*args, **kwargs)
            pdb.set_trace()
            return result
    return wrapper

@post_mortem
async def main():
    raise Exception()

asyncio.run(main())
```

How It Works

We will use a decorator solution that can be enabled via a command-line argument called --asyncio-debug or via an environment variable called CUSTOM_ASYNCIO_DEBUG which we will save in a new flag called __asyncio_ debug__.

For this matter, we define two helper methods that provide the necessary parser and check for the command-line argument/environment variable in the listed order:

```
def get_asyncio_debug_mode_parser():
    parser = argparse.ArgumentParser()
    parser.add_argument("--asyncio-debug", action="store_true",
    dest="__asyncio_debug__", default=False)
    return parser

def is_asyncio_debug_mode(parser=get_asyncio_debug_mode_parser()):
    return parser and parser.parse_args().__asyncio_debug__ or
    os.environ.get("CUSTOM_ASYNCIO_DEBUG")
```

Note   There is a Python built-in constant called __debug__. It is a globally accessible, read-only variable that is used to implement the assert mechanism. It defaults to True and can be set to False via the -O Python interpreter flag. We decided against using this mechanism since many third-party libraries wrongly use assert statements for invariants in production code. Hence, using this mechanism - the -O flag, would render their code unusable.

We initialize the __asyncio_debug__ global with a call to is_asyncio_debug_mode:

```
__asyncio_debug__ = is_asyncio_debug_mode()
```

Next, we write a coroutine/async generator decorator that respects the __asyncio_debug__ flag. In essence, it catches all not caught exceptions and uses pdp.post_mortem to give us a shell into the coroutine that threw the BaseException subclass instance.

Here, we just return the coroutine if __asyncio_debug__ is false:

```
def post_mortem(f):
    if not __asyncio_debug__:
        return f
```

In the case of an async generator function, we use async for to delegate it and wrap it with a try-except block with our pdb.post_mortem call.

We re-raise the exception to not manipulate the behavior of the coroutine.

```
if inspect.isasyncgenfunction(f):
    @wraps(f)
    async def wrapper(*args, **kwargs):
        try:
            async for payload in f(*args, **kwargs):
                yield payload
        except BaseException as err:
            pdb.post_mortem()
            raise err
```

Very similarly, we consume a coroutine with an await statement, but invoke pdb.post_mortem() on exceptions:

```
else:
    @wraps(f)
    async def wrapper(*args, **kwargs):
        try:
            return await f(*args, **kwargs)
        except BaseException as err:
            pdb.post_mortem()
            raise err

return wrapper
```

Our @pre_run decorator calls pdb.set_trace before it consumes the async generator or the coroutine function.

Other than that, the mechanism is the same as the @post_mortem decorator's mechanism:

```
def pre_run(f):
    if not __asyncio_debug__:
        return f

    if inspect.isasyncgenfunction(f):
        @wraps(f)
        async def wrapper(*args, **kwargs):
            pdb.set_trace()
            async for payload in f(*args, **kwargs):
                yield payload

    else:
        @wraps(f)
        async def wrapper(*args, **kwargs):
            pdb.set_trace()
            return await f(*args, **kwargs)

    return wrapper
```

If we are interested in the state after consuming the coroutine/async generator, we can use the @post_run decorator. Here, we can see our @post_mortem decorator in action:

```
@post_mortem
async def main():
    raise Exception()

asyncio.run(main())
```

We find ourselves inside the frame in which the exception was raised:

```
/tmp/preventing_common_asyncio_mistakes.py(94)main()
-> raise Exception()
(Pdb)
```

Writing Tests for Asyncio

Problem

We cannot rely on the execution order of a concurrently executed asyncio program to follow the order of instructions. Effects of concurrently accessing resources-like race conditions, time-related phenomena, etc. are prone to happen in asyncio applications and cannot be covered by testing measures that are "not aware" of coroutines.

Solution

The term "software-testing" in the context of this chapter is "software that is able to deterministically assert that other software behaves as specified". Software testing can be conducted on many levels, as follows (in the order of descending granularity):

- Unit testing
- Integration testing
- System testing

All these still have the goal in common that they want to "deterministically assert that other software behaves as specified". Here, we'll focus on the role of *unit testing* since it is the most common.

Picking the right assertions that the tests must ensure becomes more critical in the context of concurrency. Furthermore, it dictates in a way how the concurrent code is written. It implies the need for invariants that hold true irrespective of the concurrent nature of the program. For instance, testing timing-related properties of a concurrent program does not make much sense to ensure its correctness.

To help us with that, we can use packages like pytest, pytest-asyncio, doctest, and asynctest. For this solution, we write our own unittest.TestCase subclass that allows us to test coroutines. We also learn how to deal with the unittest.mock.patch API around coroutines to intercept calls to asyncio.sleep or stdout output.

```python
import asyncio
import functools
from io import StringIO
from unittest import TestCase, main as unittest_main
from unittest.mock import patch

def into_future(arg, *, loop=None):
    fut = (loop or asyncio.get_running_loop()).create_future()
    fut.set_exception(arg) if isinstance(arg, Exception) else \
    fut.set_result(arg)
    return fut

class AsyncTestCase(TestCase):
    def __getattribute__(self, name):
        attr = super().__getattribute__(name)
        if name.startswith('test') and asyncio.
        iscoroutinefunction(attr):
            return functools.partial(asyncio.run, attr())
        else:
            return attr

class AsyncTimer:
    async def execute_timely(self, delay, times, f, *args,
    **kwargs):
```

```
        for i in range(times):
            await asyncio.sleep(delay)
            (await f(*args, **kwargs)) if asyncio.
            iscoroutine(f) else f(*args, **kwargs)

class AsyncTimerTest(AsyncTestCase):

    async def test_execute_timely(self):
        times = 3
        delay = 3

        with  patch("asyncio.sleep", return_value=into_
                    future(None)) as mock_sleep, \
               patch('sys.stdout', new_callable=StringIO) as
               mock_stdout:
            async_timer = AsyncTimer()
            await async_timer.execute_timely(delay, times,
            print, "test_execute_timely")

        mock_sleep.assert_called_with(delay)
        assert mock_stdout.getvalue() == "test_execute_timely\
        ntest_execute_timely\ntest_execute_timely\n"

if __name__ == '__main__':
    unittest_main()
```

How It Works

We will start with our imports:

```
import asyncio
import functools
```

We are importing functools to enable the TestCase subclasses to run coroutine test methods.

```
from io import StringIO
```

StringIO will be used to intercept the stdout output.

```
from unittest import TestCase, main as unittest_main
```

We import the TestCase class to provide an async one, which can test coroutine methods. We also import unittest.main under an alias to put it into an if __name__ == '__main__' guard. Every time this class is invoked as the first script, all our test cases will run.

```
from unittest.mock import patch
```

We also import the unittest.mock.path function, which we will use to intercept asyncio.sleep and everything printed to stdout. Next, we write a helper that wraps an argument into an future, which we will use to mock out asyncio.sleep.

```
def into_future(arg, *, loop=None):
    fut = (loop or asyncio.get_running_loop()).create_future()
    fut.set_exception(arg) if isinstance(arg, Exception) else
    fut.set_result(arg)
    return fut
```

The TestCase class of the unittest module provides APIs for unit testing by declaring synchronous methods that start with test. You cannot use coroutine methods as of now. So we subclass the TestCase class to be able to intercept every attribute access to the respective test methods. If the user tries to access a method of the AsyncTestCase class whose name starts with "test", we need to wrap the requested method into a partial that can schedule the coroutine in a synchronous fashion. For this matter, we use functools.partial to provide a callable, which wraps the coroutine inside asnycio.run.

```
class AsyncTestCase(TestCase):
    def __getattribute__(self, name):
        attr = super().__getattribute__(name)
        if name.startswith('test') and asyncio.
        iscoroutinefunction(attr):
            return functools.partial(asyncio.run, attr())
        else:
            return attr
```

Next, we write a simple class called AsyncTimer that we will unit test. The class has only one method, called execute_timely, which schedules a (coroutine) function multiple times and adds a delay in between the calls via asyncio.sleep. execute_timely accepts functions, coroutine functions, and arguments passed after the function are passed through (to the scheduled coroutine function/function). The method has parameters to tweak how often the function/coroutine function is called and how long the delay is called delay and times.

```
class AsyncTimer:
    async def execute_timely(self, delay, times, f, *args,
    **kwargs):
        for i in range(times):
            await asyncio.sleep(delay)
            (await f(*args, **kwargs)) if asyncio.
            iscoroutine(f) else f(*args, **kwargs)
```

Next, we write an AsyncTestCase subclass to test AsyncTimer. We will call the subclass AsyncTimerTest. Since we have altered the behavior of __getattribute__ inside of AsyncTestCase to wrap all test coroutine methods on our AsyncTestCase class into partials, we can use the await keyword with asyncio.run inside of test_execute_timely. Prefixing the name with test ensures that the test will be executed if we invoke the unit test runner on this file.

```
class AsyncTimerTest(AsyncTestCase):
    async def test_execute_timely(self):
        times = 3
        delay = 3
```

We declare the class and the test coroutine method with the correct name and set up two variables that determine how often the passed (coroutine) function is scheduled and how long the time is in between.

```
    with  patch("asyncio.sleep", return_value=into_
                future(None)) as mock_sleep, \
            patch('sys.stdout', new_callable=StringIO) as
            mock_stdout:
        async_timer = AsyncTimer()
        await async_timer.execute_timely(delay, times,
        print, "test_execute_timely")
```

Using unittest.mock.path, we now can intercept all calls to asyncio. sleep. To do so, we need the return value of our mock function to be an awaitable since asyncio.sleep is being awaited in AsyncTimer.execute_ timely. The return_value we pass is an empty future where the result is already set (in this case, it is None because the return value of asyncio. sleep is not used). Why? Because when the result is already set on a future, it returns immediately upon awaiting. The resulting behavior is that awaiting our patched versions of asyncio.sleep causes await asyncio. sleep to return directly. Next, we patch sys.stdout to be a StringIO instance. This way, we can intercept every print call that was made:

```
    mock_sleep.assert_called_with(delay)
    assert mock_stdout.getvalue() == "test_execute_timely\
    ntest_execute_timely\ntest_execute_timely\n"
```

Using our mock objects, we can assert now that asyncio.sleep was indeed called with **delay** seconds *and* that test_execute_timely\ntest_execute_timely was printed three times on stdout.

```
if __name__ == '__main__':
    unittest_main()
```

Last but not least, we called our aliased unittest.main function to make it easier to run the unit test. All we need to do is to run this file and our test cases will be discovered.

Writing Tests for Pytest (Using Pytest-Asyncio)

Problem

We want to write unit tests for asyncio with less boilerplate code.

Solution

Python 3 includes the unittest standard library module, which does a good job at giving us an interface for writing unit tests in the Python language. Pytest is a third-party package that helps us write unit tests with less boilerplate code involved. Using Pytest and pytest-asyncio, we will create a simple example to test coroutines.

You need to install pytest via your package manager of choice. For example, via pip or pipenv:

```
pip3 install pytest==3.8.0
pip3 install pytest-asyncio==0.9.0

# or
```

```
pipenvinstall pytest==3.8.0
pipenv install pytest-asyncio==0.9.0

import asyncio
import sys
from types import SimpleNamespace

import pytest

def check_pytest_asyncio_installed():
    import os
    from importlib import util
    if not util.find_spec("pytest_asyncio"):
        print("You need to install pytest-asyncio first!",
        file=sys.stderr)
        sys.exit(os.EX_SOFTWARE)

async def return_after_sleep(res):
    return await asyncio.sleep(2, result=res)

async def setattr_async(loop, delay, ns, key, payload):
    loop.call_later(delay, setattr, ns, key, payload)

@pytest.fixture()
async def loop():
    return asyncio.get_running_loop()

@pytest.fixture()
def namespace():
    return SimpleNamespace()

@pytest.mark.asyncio
async def test_return_after_sleep():
    expected_result = b'expected result'
    res = await return_after_sleep(expected_result)
    assert expected_result == res
```

```
@pytest.mark.asyncio
async def test_setattr_async(loop, namespace):
    key = "test"
    delay = 1.0
    expected_result = object()
    await setattr_async(loop, delay, namespace, key, expected_
    result)
    await asyncio.sleep(delay)
    assert getattr(namespace, key, None) is expected_result

if __name__ == '__main__':
    check_pytest_asyncio_installed()
    pytest.main(sys.argv)
```

How It Works

We define a helper function that asserts that we have the pytest-asyncio plugin installed:

```
def check_pytest_asyncio_installed():
    import os
    from importlib import util
    if not util.find_spec("pytest_asyncio"):
        print("You need to install pytest-asyncio first!",
        file=sys.stderr)
        sys.exit(os.EX_SOFTWARE)
```

It checks for the existence of the module without importing via importlib.

Next, we define coroutine functions we want to test:

```
async def return_after_sleep(res):
    return await asyncio.sleep(2, result=res)
```

```
async def write_async(loop, delay, ns, key, payload):
    loop.call_later(delay, setattr, ns, key, payload)
```

The @pytest.fixture decorator allows us to inject parameters into the test functions on every new run.

Using the pytest-asyncio module, it also supports coroutine functions:

```
@pytest.fixture()
async def loop():
    return asyncio.get_running_loop()
```

Since it runs in the context of a running loop, we can query the running loop via asyncio.get_running_loop and inject it into our test functions. Our first simple test asserts that the resulting value of our function is equal to the one given as input:

```
@pytest.mark.asyncio
async def test_return_after_sleep():
    expected_result = b'expected result'
    res = await return_after_sleep(expected_result)
    assert expected_result == res
```

Next, we ensure that our write_async function does in fact set an attribute asynchronously given a specific delay. To await the delay, we use asyncio.sleep as opposed to time.sleep to not block the coroutine. After the delay, we assert that the attribute was indeed set.

```
@pytest.mark.asyncio
async def test_setattr_async(loop, namespace):
    key = "test"
    delay = 1.0
    expected_result = object()
    await setattr_async(loop, delay, namespace, key, expected_
    result)
```

```
await asyncio.sleep(delay)
assert getattr(namespace, key, None) is expected_result
```

To make this example easier to execute, we defined a __main__ hook for easier script usage:

```
if __name__ == '__main__':
    check_pytest_asyncio_installed()
    pytest.main(sys.argv)
```

Writing Tests for Asynctest

Problem

This example solves the problem of knowing whether your coroutine was awaited and with which arguments, etc.

Solution

Seasoned Pythonists know that the standard library module unittest provides a patch context manager that can help mock objects and functions. The third-party module asynctest provides a CoroutineMock object (among other features) that we can use to integrate our coroutines with the unittest mock API. For this example, you need to install it via your package manager of choice, such as pip or pipenv:

```
pip3 install asynctest==0.12.2
pip3 install asynctest==0.12.2

# or

pipenvinstall asynctest==0.12.2
pipenv install asynctest==0.12.2
```

Using the `asynctest` module's `CoroutineMock` object and the mock context manager of the `unittest` module, we can intercept calls to our coroutine object and its return values.

```python
import sys
from unittest.mock import patch

import asynctest
import pytest

def check_pytest_asyncio_installed():
    import os
    from importlib import util
    if not util.find_spec("pytest_asyncio"):
        print("You need to install pytest-asyncio first!",
        file=sys.stderr)
        sys.exit(os.EX_SOFTWARE)

async def printer(*args, printfun, **kwargs):
    printfun(*args, kwargs)

async def async_printer(*args, printcoro, printfun, **kwargs):
    await printcoro(*args, printfun=printfun, **kwargs)

@pytest.mark.asyncio
async def test_printer_with_print():
    text = "Hello world!"
    dict_of_texts = dict(more_text="This is a nested text!")

    with patch('builtins.print') as mock_printfun:
        await printer(text, printfun=mock_printfun, **dict_of_
        texts)
        mock_printfun.assert_called_once_with(text, dict_of_
        texts)
```

```
@pytest.mark.asyncio
async def test_async_printer_with_print():
    text = "Hello world!"
    dict_of_texts = dict(more_text="This is a nested text!")
    with patch('__main__.printer', new=asynctest.
    CoroutineMock()) as mock_printfun:
        await async_printer(text, printcoro=mock_printfun,
        printfun=print, **dict_of_texts)
        mock_printfun.assert_called_once_with(text,
        printfun=print, **dict_of_texts)

if __name__ == '__main__':
    check_pytest_asyncio_installed()
    pytest.main(sys.argv)
```

How It works

We skip our check_pytest_asyncio_installed helper since we have defined the function in the upper example. First, we define the coroutine functions to be tested.

Note   We designed the helper coroutine functions to illustrate how to use asynctest.CoroutineMock but not to be useful beyond that purpose.

Here, we basically pass all arguments nearly unaltered to printfun (besides not unpacking kwargs):

```
async def printer(*args, printfun, **kwargs):
    printfun(*args, kwargs)
```

And analogue for `async_printer` as follows:

```
async def async_printer(*args, printcoro, printfun, **kwargs):
    await printcoro(*args, printfun=printfun, **kwargs)
```

We know from the last section that we can run coroutine test functions in pytest with the `pytest-asyncio` plugin:

```
@pytest.mark.asyncio
async def test_printer_with_print():
    text = "Hello world!"
    dict_of_texts = dict(more_text="This is a nested text!")
```

Using `unittest.patch`, we can mock the `print` built-in. Using the identifier `builtins.print`, we can use the instance stored in the `builtins` module and pass it (instead of `print`) as the `printfun` parameter.

`mock_printfun` is a proxy object that delegates the call to the original implementation and exposes methods that we can use to view what happened inside of it. For instance, we use the `mock.assert_called_once_with` method to see if `mock_printfun` was indeed passed the arguments as we would expect:

```
    with patch('builtins.print') as mock_printfun:
        await printer(text, printfun=mock_printfun, **dict_of_
        texts)
        mock_printfun.assert_called_once_with(text, dict_of_
        texts)
```

We can similarly check in the coroutine case if the arguments where passed correctly by passing an `asynctest.CoroutineMock` instance to the path function:

```
    with patch('__main__.printer', new=asynctest.
CoroutineMock()) as mock_printfun:
```

Note   We need to name the printer `__main__.printer` because we have defined the function in the same document as the script we use for running.

After awaiting `async_printer`, we can check if the patched coroutine `mock_printfun` was indeed called with the correct arguments:

```
await async_printer(text, printcoro=mock_printfun,
printfun=print, **dict_of_texts)
        mock_printfun.assert_called_once_with(text,
        printfun=print, **dict_of_texts)
```

`asynctest.CoroutineMock` exposes more APIs, which you can look up on the offical GitHub page at `https://github.com/Martiusweb/asynctest`.

Writing Tests for Doctest

Problem

We want to write interactive tests inline inside the Python docstring.

Solution

Doctest is a neat tool in the standard library, but it's not well known among Python developers. It provides a convenient interface to write interactive tests inline inside the Python docstring. Its uses, according to the documentation, are three-fold:

- To check that a module's docstrings are up-to-date

- To perform regression testing

- To write interactive tutorial documentation for a package

In this solution, the doctest module will be used to test the function called complicated.

```
async def complicated(a,b,c):
    """

    >>> import asyncio
    >>> asyncio.run(complicated(5,None,None))
    True
    >>> asyncio.run(complicated(None,None,None))
    Traceback (most recent call last):

        ...

    ValueError: This value: None is not an int or larger than 4
    >>> asyncio.run(complicated(None,"This","will be printed
    out"))
    This will be printed out

    :param a: This parameter controls the return value
    :param b:
    :param c:
    :return:
    """

    if isinstance(a,int) and a > 4:
        return True
    elif b and c:
        print(b,c)
    else:
        raise ValueError(f"This value: {a} is not an int or
        larger than 4")

if __name__ == "__main__":
    import doctest
    doctest.testmod()
```

How It Works

Since doctest mimics an interactive interpreter, we cannot just use awaits inside of it. Instead, we can asyncio.run wherever an await is needed.

First, we import asyncio:

```
"""
>>> import asyncio
```

Next, we use asyncio.run to schedule the coroutine and (since it returns the return value) write the result on the next line:

```
>>> asyncio.run(complicated(5,None,None))
True
```

In the case of an exception we write the following:

```
Traceback (most recent call last):
    ...
```

Then the representation (given by __repr__) of the exception:

```
ValueError: This value: None is not an int or larger than 4
```

The next important bit is some convenience code used to run the file's documentation tests if they run as a script:

```
if __name__ == "__main__":
    import doctest
    doctest.testmod()
```

APPENDIX A

Setting Up Your Environment

Choosing the correct tools to work with asyncio is a non-trivial choice, since it can significantly impact the availability and performance of asyncio. In this appendix, we discuss the interpreter and the packaging options that influence your asyncio experience.

The Interpreter

Depending on the API version of the interpreter, the syntax of declaring coroutines change and the suggestions considering API usage change. (Passing the loop parameter is considered deprecated for APIs newer than 3.6, instantiating your own loop should happen only in rare circumstances in Python 3.7, etc.)

Availability

Python interpreters adhere to the standard in varying degrees. This is because they are implementations/manifestations of the Python language specification, which is managed by the PSF.

At the time of this writing, three relevant interpreters support at least parts of asyncio out of the box: CPython, MicroPython, and PyPy.

© Mohamed Mustapha Tahrioui 2019
M. M. Tahrioui, *asyncio Recipes*, https://doi.org/10.1007/978-1-4842-4401-2

Since we are ideally interested in a complete or semi-complete implementation of asyncio, our choice is limited to CPython and PyPy. Both of these products have a great community.

Since we are ideally using a lot powerful `stdlib` features, it is inevitable to pose the question of implementation completeness of a given interpreter with respect to the Python specification.

The CPython interpreter is the reference implementation of the language specification and hence it adheres to the largest set of features in the language specification. At the point of this writing, CPython was targeting API version 3.7.

PyPy is a close second, but it's a third-party implementation and therefore adopts new features a bit slower. At the point of this writing, PyPy was targeting API version 3.5 (or just in alpha quality).

Performance

Since asyncio is implementation dependent, CPython and PyPy can yield substantially different performance footprints. For example, a program using `aiohttp` (an asyncio library for interaction over the HTTP protocol) and running on PyPy overpowers an instance running on CPython after the fourth second in terms of requests per seconds, by magnitudes up to 6.2.

Summing It Up

For the sake of this book, we give precedence to feature completeness. Therefore, we use CPython release 3.7.0. You can find the interpreter that matches your OS environment here:

`https://www.python.org/downloads/release/python-370/`

For reproducible installs, you may choose to follow the rest of this appendix.

The Setup

At the time of this writing, Python is shipped by most *nix operating systems. However, that version probably will not satisfy our needs.

There are concerns about pre-3.7 versions. Versions 3.3-3.4 expose a decorator-based API for declaring coroutines and for yielding control back to the event loop.

As the changelog indicates, there are fixes included in the 3.7.0 version that address serious issues like the following:

- bpo-33674: Fixed a race condition in `SSLProtocol.connection_made()` of `asyncio.sslproto`: start the handshake immediately instead of using `call_soon()`. Previously, `data_received()` could be called before the handshake started, causing the handshake to hang or fail.

- bpo-32841: Fixed an `asyncio.Condition` issue, which silently ignored cancellation after notifying and cancelling a conditional lock.

- bpo-32734: Fixed an `asyncio.Lock()` safety issue, which allowed acquiring and locking the same lock multiple times, without it being free.

- bpo-26133: Don't unsubscribe signals in an asyncio UNIX event loop upon interpreter shutdown.

- bpo-27585: Fixed waiter cancellation in `asyncio.Lock`.

- bpo-31061: Fixed a crash when using asyncio and threads.

- bpo-30828: Fixed an out-of-bounds write in `asyncio.CFuture.remove_done_callback()`.

Windows

The Windows operation system does not come with a Python version installed. Python 2 support is better for newer versions of Python 2 and Windows:

> *"[…] Up to 2.5, Python was still compatible with Windows 95, 98 and ME (but already raised a deprecation warning on installation). For Python 2.6 (and all following releases), this support was dropped, and new releases are just expected to work on the Windows NT family. [...]"*

Source: `https://docs.python.org/2/using/windows.html`

For Python 3, the official statement is:

> *"As specified in PEP 11, a Python release only supports a Windows platform while Microsoft considers the platform under extended support. This means that Python 3.6 supports Windows Vista and newer. If you require Windows XP support, then please install Python 3.4."*

Source: `https://docs.python.org/3/using/windows.html`

This means to run Python 3.7.0, you have to run Windows Vista.

Installing Python 3.7.0 on Vista

Browse to `https://www.python.org/downloads/release/python-370/` or find the link to the Windows x86-64 executable installer here:

`https://www.python.org/ftp/python/3.7.0/python-3.7.0-amd64.exe`

After the download, make sure the `MD5` sums match via this command:

`CertUtil -hashfile python-3.7.0-amd64.exe MD5`

If it matches the one on the website, proceed with the installation. Otherwise, redo the procedure.

Follow the installation procedure and make sure to add the home folder of your Python installation to the path. Python 3.7.0 is usually installed under C:\Python37.

Installing Python 3.7.0 on Windows 7+

The recommended way to install Python 3.6 on Windows 7+ is to use Chocolatey. Chocolatey is a community system package manager for Windows 7+. It is something like apt-get/pacman/yast2 in Linux distributions or brew on MacOS X.

You can read about Chocolatey's installation procedure here:

```
https://chocolatey.org/docs/installation
```

To install Python 3, we specify the correct package when invoking Chocolatey like so:

```
choco install python -version 3.7.0
```

Once Chocolatey runs, you should be able to launch Python directly from the console since Chocolatey adds it to the path automatically.

Setuptools and Pip

To be able to download, install, and uninstall any compliant Python software product, you need setuptools and pip. This way, you can install third-party Python packages with a single command. Also, they allow you to enable network installation capabilities on our own Python software with just a little work. All supported versions of Python 3 include pip, so just make sure it's up to date:

```
python -m pip install -U pip
```

MacOS

MacOS users are presented with an outdated Python 2.7 version, which we cannot use with asyncio:

> *"MacOS X 10.8 comes with Python 2.7 pre-installed by Apple. If you wish, you are invited to install the most recent version of Python 3 from the Python website (`https://www.python.org`). A current "universal binary" build of Python, which runs natively on the Mac's new Intel and legacy PPC CPU's, is available there."*

Source: `https://docs.python.org/3/using/mac.html`

This means we can pretty much run Python 3.7.0 on newer MacOS X versions. The recommend way to install Python 3.7.0 is to install it via `brew`, which is a community system package manager for MacOS X. It is something like `apt-get/pacman/yast2` in Linux distributions.

`brew` can be used to install the Python distribution of our choice. You can find it under `https://brew.sh` or, at the time of this writing, you can use this code snippet:

```
$ /usr/bin/ruby -e "$(curl -fsSL https://raw.githubusercontent.com/Homebrew/install/master/install)"
```

Make sure the packages installed by `brew` are the first ones to be recognized by your system:

```
export PATH="/usr/local/bin:/usr/local/sbin:$PATH"
```

Install the Python distribution of our choice. Since we want to specifically install the Python 3.7.0 version, just doing the following will result in irreproducible configurations, which we want to avoid:

```
$ brew install python
```

We can instead refer to the commit version more explicitly (which will install the Python 3.7.0 version to our system) by issuing:

```
$ brew install https://raw.githubusercontent.com/Homebrew/
homebrew-core/82038e3b6de9d162c7987b8f2f60d8f538591f15/Formula/
python.rb
```

The Python installation by default comes with `pip` and `setuptools` included, so you are ready to go. To test it, you may execute the following:

```
$ which python3
```

Which should yield the following:

```
/usr/local/bin/python3
```

Executing this:

```
$ python3
```

Should yield (besides the second line, which depends on your Xcode toolchain) the following:

```
Python 3.7.0 (default, <current date>)
[GCC 4.2.1 Compatible Apple LLVM 8.0.0 (clang-800.0.42.1)] on
darwin
Type "help", "copyright", "credits" or "license" for more
information.
>>>
```

Linux

Linux users may find a Python 3 version installed on their operation systems. For example, Debian flavors ship with versions ranging from 3.3 to 3.5 (Jessy - Stretch), which are all unacceptable for our asyncio use

case. To install the CPython 3.7.0 release version on Debian flavors, add
deadsnakes ppa and install Python 3.7.0 like this:

```
$ sudo apt-get install software-properties-common
$ sudo add-apt-repository ppa:deadsnakes/ppa
$ sudo apt-get update
$ sudo apt-get install python3.7
```

Note   This will install a global version of the Python interpreter on
your system.

Debian-based systems have an update-alternatives mechanism, which
you can use to ensure the system picks the right interpreter. You can list all
the possible alternatives for a tool like so:

```
$ update-alternatives --list python
```

You can install a new version like so:

```
$ update-alternatives --install /usr/bin/python python /usr/
bin/python3.7 1
```

Where 1 is the priority (a higher score means more significance) and /
usr/bin/python is the symlink target.

To install pip, do not pick the version provided by your system packaging
tools. Rather, download it manually, as described on the official page:

```
curl https://bootstrap.pypa.io/get-pip.py -o get-pip.py

python get-pip.py
```

You may choose to update it from time to time via this command:

```
pip install -U pip
```

The testing procedure for a Linux distribution is the same as the
MacOS one.

APPENDIX B

Event Loops

An *event* is a message that is emitted in a certain condition by one part of the program. A *loop,* on the other hand, is a construct that finishes under a certain condition and executes a certain program until it does so.

An *event loop* therefore is a loop that allows one to subscribe to the event transmission and register handlers/callbacks. It enables the program to run in an asynchronous fashion. The event loop delegates all the events it receives to their respective callbacks.

Most implementations of callback patterns have one major drawback: they dictate the programming style in a way that introduces a lot of nesting. This happens because the execution of synchronous code follows the order of its instructions.

Hence, to express that certain parts of a program depend on each other, we use ordering. In the case of dependence on an asynchronous result, however, the following patterns have evolved:

- Nesting callbacks, so that the inner callback can access the outer callback's results (closures)

- Using objects that act as proxies of a future result (so-called *futures* or *promises*)

- Coroutines, which are suspendible functions that run in event loops

© Mohamed Mustapha Tahrioui 2019
M. M. Tahrioui, *asyncio Recipes*, https://doi.org/10.1007/978-1-4842-4401-2

Nesting Callbacks

The rule of thumb for nesting callbacks is that if there is a need to wait for the result of a callback, it is necessary to embed your code inside the respective callback. You quickly end up with a situation that is infamously coined *callback hell.* Callback hell is the point where the depth of the callback nesting makes reasoning and improving the program a maintenance nightmare.

Futures/Promises

Futures or promises are objects that encapsulate the result and error handling of an asynchronous call.

They eventually provide APIs to query the current state of the results/exceptions and ways to register a callback for handling results/exceptions.

Since they encapsulate the future context of the asynchronous call and need nesting, the resulting program appears to be written in a more top-down fashion.

Coroutines

You can think of *coroutines* as suspendible functions.

Being suspendible means that we can pause the coroutine at any given point. This means there must be some sort of atomic unit that it consists of.

This is what we might refer to and measure as a *tick.* A tick is the time unit of the event loop. It encompasses all the actions that happen in one iteration step of the event loop.

Coroutines can in fact do more: they can suspend themselves and await the result of another coroutine.

All the logic behind the waiting is coordinated by the event loop since it is aware of the respective coroutine state.

The Lifecycle of Event Loops in Asyncio

Event loops in asyncio have four states they can be in:

- Idle

- Running

- Stopped

- Closed

You can interact with the lifecycle of the event loop by means of four event loop methods, which can be split into starting, stopping, and closing methods.

They constitute the event loop lifecycle interface that all asyncio/third-party event loops need to provide for compatibility:

- `run_forever`

- `run_until_complete`

The `run_forever` method is called without a parameter, whereas the `run_until_complete` method consumes a coroutine. To stop, we use the `stop` method and to close, we use the `close` method.

The Idle State

The idle state is the state the loop is in after creation. It cannot consume any coroutine or any callback in this state.

In this state, `loop.is_running` returns the value `False`.

The Running State

The running state is the state the loop is in after either calling `loop.run_forever` or `loop.run_until_complete`.

In this state, the loop.is_running method returns the value True.

The difference between the methods is that, in the case of loop. run_until_complete, the coroutine—passed as an argument to loop. run_until_complete—is wrapped in an asyncio.Future.

A callback is registered as a handler on the asyncio.Future object that runs the loop.stop method after the coroutine is fully consumed.

The Stopped State

The stopped state is the state the loop is in after calling the stop command.

The loop does not return False for the is_running method just after calling the stop method.

Any batch of pending callbacks are consumed first. Only after they are consumed does the loop move into the idle state.

Note Callbacks scheduled after calling loop.stop will be disregarded/not scheduled. Instead, they are executed when the event loop moves back into a running state.

The Closed State

The loop enters the closed state by calling the close method. It can only be called if the loop is not in the running state. The documentation states further that it:

"[..] clears the queues and shuts down the executor but does not wait for the executor to finish. It is idempotent and irreversible. No other methods should be called after this one."

Basic Classes for Event Loops

There are two options for shipping your own event loops in Python 3. Abstract event loops are provided by the `asyncio.events` and `asyncio.base_events` modules. `AbstractEventLoop` and `BaseEventLoop` represent two potential classes for an event loop implementation.

AbstractEventLoop

The `AbstractEventLoop` class defines the interface of an event loop in the asyncio ecosystem. The interface methods can be roughly split into the following sections:

- Lifecycle methods (running, stopping, querying the state of, and closing the loop)

- Scheduling methods

- Callbacks

- Coroutines

- Future creation

- Thread-related methods

- I/O-related methods

- Low-level APIs (socket, pipe, and reader/writer APIs)

- High-level APIs (server, pipe, and subprocess-related methods)

- Signal methods

- Debug flag management methods

The API is stable and can be subclassed in the case of a manual event loop implementation.

BaseEventLoop

Despite being more high-level component based, the `BaseEventLoop` class should not be used to create a manual loop implementation because its API is not stable. But it can be used as guidance on how to implement one.

Its `BaseEventLoop._run_once` method is called on every tick of the loop and therefore encompasses all the actions needed in one iteration.

This calls all currently ready callbacks, polls for I/O, schedules the resulting callbacks, and then schedules `call_later` callbacks.

If you plan to implement an event loop yourself, you will need to provide a method that's similar to it. The name and body of the function are just implementation details.

Are Event Loops OS Specific?

Yes, event loops are OS specific. This may affect API availability and the speed of the event loop. For instance, `add_signal_handler` and `remove_signal_handler` are UNIX-only loop APIs.

One of the reasons behind the OS specificity—besides missing corresponding native bindings—is that most of the loops are implemented based on the `selectors` module.

The `selectors` module provides a high-level I/O multiplexing interface based on the `select` module. The `selectors` module is built on top of `Select`, `poll`, `devpoll`, `epoll`, or `kqueue`, depending on the underlying OS. The block in the `selectors` module is responsible for setting `DefaultSelector`, which in turn is used by the asyncio module (see Listing B-1).

Listing B-1. Selectors Selection in the Selectors Module

```
if 'KqueueSelector' in globals():
    DefaultSelector = KqueueSelector
elif 'EpollSelector' in globals():
    DefaultSelector = EpollSelector
elif 'DevpollSelector' in globals():
    DefaultSelector = DevpollSelector
elif 'PollSelector' in globals():
    DefaultSelector = PollSelector
else:
    DefaultSelector = SelectSelector
```

Note   Windows also has a `ProactorEventLoop` implementation that is based on I/O completion ports or short IOCP.

The official documentation of IOCP describes them as "an efficient threading model for processing multiple asynchronous I/O requests on a multiprocessor system".

The `ProactorEventLoop` may, for example, be used on Windows if the need arises to use the asyncio subprocess APIs. See `https://www.python.org/downloads/release/python-370/`.

Index

A

© Mohamed Mustapha Tahrioui 2019
M. M. Tahrioui, *asyncio Recipes*, https://doi.org/10.1007/978-1-4842-4401-2

U, V

T

W, X

Printed in the United States
By Bookmasters